HANOI OF A THOUSAND YEARS

Books by the same author

Dragons on the Roof, Unravelling Vietnam
Secrets of Hoi An, Vietnam's Historic Port
Hue, Vietnam's Last Imperial Capital

Carol Howland is an experienced travel writer, a former feature writer for a national magazine and a contributor to more than a dozen British newspapers. Following a mid-career foray into stockbroking, she edited two finance magazines. But early in her career, she wrote and revised guidebooks and more recently, returned to travel writing. Enthralled by the country, she has published four books exploring Vietnam's cultural heritage. She now lives in France.

'Carol Howland has written four travel books, that had they been written and read by the intelligentsia of America before the Vietnam War, would have made the US pause and take stock of the state of affairs in this small, now well-known country.

'The author's meticulous research into the customs, traditions and cultural history of Vietnam are a mind opening revelation to the uninitiated traveller. She explores the exotic venues of an historically turbulent culture that is vibrantly alive and growing in spite of today's conflicts among the powerful nations of the world.

'Reading her series of books on Vietnam, *Dragons on the Roof, Hanoi of a Thousand Years, Hoi An – Vietnam's Historic Port* and *Hue – Vietnam's Last Imperial Capital,* is a deeply rewarding experience. Without even mentioning the Vietnam War, she leads the reader on a journey through the cities and countryside of this beautiful Asian country and the mysterious mindset of the proud, persistent and independent people of Vietnam. Her descriptions of the ancient civilizations in the early years and how the country developed through Taoism, Confucianism, Hinduism, Buddhism, and Catholicism leave the reader with an astounding wealth of information to synthesize in order to appreciate the varieties of experience one can expect when visiting this country.

'From the tale of the two Vietnamese Trung sisters who repulsed the An Chinese in 40 AD through the expulsion of Kublai Khan, the Japanese in WWII, the French Colonialists, and infamously, the US, to the beautiful flower gardens, architecture, cuisine of the rich and poor, to the type of jewellery worn in the imperial court of Hue, she writes in great detail of the marvels of manners and grace still apparent in the Vietnamese people.

'First published in Hanoi by Vietnam's publisher of foreign language books, her books celebrate Vietnamese culture, a remarkable series of books that elucidate the many faces of Vietnam. Her wit, insights and thoroughness permeate the writing and bring joy, excitement and expectation to the would be traveller and historian. Read them, go to Vietnam, and follow her suggestions to have a really rewarding experience in Vietnam!'

Ken Embers, Vietnam representative for Globalism; Director of English Programs and Projects for Vietnam Children's Libraries International; Captain, helicopter pilot, Vietnam 1968-69.

'Like a military reporter, Carol Howland embeds herself with her subject. However, her strategy is less military than empathy and Howland has not only the gift of insight but the gift of friendship: she leaves her subjects like a long lost pal, a priceless asset in this big hearted but still endlessly enigmatic country.'

Peter Howick, Columnist, *The Evening Herald,* Dublin

HANOI
OF A THOUSAND YEARS

CAROL HOWLAND

MYNAH BIRD BOOKS

Published by Mynah Bird Books 2018
1 Regents Court, 10 Balcombe Road
Branksome Park, Poole, Dorset BH13 6DY

First published 2009 by The Gioi Publishers,
46 Tran Hung Dao Street
Hanoi, Vietnam

ISBN – 13: 978-1-999843618
ISBN – 10: 1999843614

To Vietnamese scholar, Huu Ngoc,
without whose numeous books
this one could not have been written,
and to my Buddhist friend, who
provided much enlightenment.

CONTENTS

BIRTH OF A CITY

A hundred things heard are not worth one seen
– Vietnamese proverb

Hanoi feels like a *millefeuille* of a city, built layer upon layer of history. Its triangular core of tightly packed shop houses locked in a triangle by rivers and lakes, contrasts with the gracious, broad leafy avenues, elaborate villas and ostentatious government buildings of the French colonial era and the sleek new towers that have shot up in the past decade.

But what sets Hanoi apart from other Asian, or for that matter, Indo-Chinese cities such as Vientiane, Phnom Penh or even Saigon (Ho Chi Minh City), is how openly yet discretely it displays its past, like a dowager wearing old lace, exposing a few old bones here and there in the form of its most venerable, often quietly tucked-away temples and pagodas.

Or perhaps one should say, Hanoi's many pasts: pre-historic tribal capital, regional trading outpost as a vassal state, feudal imperial capital, provincial capital, French colonial headquarters, and finally, capital of an independent country – in 2010, glorying in the one thousandth anniversary of its founding in 1010 as a capital city called the Flying Dragon (Thang Long).

Throughout its dramatic history, Hanoi has born many names: Giao Chi (Remote Land), Tong Binh (Proper Home), An Nam (Pacified South – of China), Dai La (Great Belt, as in the dyke surrounding the city), Dong Do and Dong Quan (both meaning Capital), Dong Kinh (Eastern Capital), which French priests later transformed into Tonquin and Tonkin. The name Hanoi only appeared after the Nguyen dynasty attained power in 1802, shifted the capital to Hue and renamed the city in 1831. Hanoi translates variously as city in the river, city surrounded by rivers, city in the bend of the river, or more romantically, as city in the embrace of the river. Despite the name change, until well into the twentieth century, people continued to call it Thang Long. Some still do. And here and there, a restaurant or a hotel still preserves the old name.

Returning to Hanoi for me is always like returning to a second home, but a second home in another world, in another existence. It is a city that remembers well it past and revels in its glories. Although at every turn, at every glance, it is a city in a rush to develop.

With an estimated population of 3.2 million (2008) and a population density of 3,402 people to the square mile (1,225 to the sq km), Hanoi is one of the most densely populated cities in Asia and the capital of one of South East Asia's most vibrant young tiger economies.

Underlying Vietnam's reverence for the past is the collective ancestor worship of the Viet or Kinh people, who make up 87 per cent of Vietnam's population of 84.1 million – two-thirds of whom are under thirty. This respect for ancestors extends well beyond the family to village deities, to founders of craft guilds, as well as to literary, military and political heroes. And because the Vietnamese have always welcomed new religions as they came along, to the Taoist, Confucian and Buddhist religious deities of China and India as well. These collective memories of eminent historic and sometimes mythological personages remain omnipresent in the names of Hanoi's streets, statues, parks and lakes, not forgetting the multitude of dedicatees honoured in the city's literally hundreds of temples and community houses.

This reverence for heroes of the past enables us to reach back through the generations, through the dynasties, through the millennia to the shadowy beginnings of the Vietnamese – several tribes called Lac and Viet, living in what is now north-west Vietnam, south of the Yangtze River.

By the end of the third century BC, they had united to form a mini-state called Au Lac and established the Hung dynasty, which lasted through eighteen kings, its ancient capital at Co Loa, twelve miles (20 km) north of Hanoi. Vietnam is rich in myth and legend, the result of the long oral tradition of a long illiterate people, apart from a few scholars.

When I first came to Hanoi in 1997, agog off a cruise liner with only four hours to devour the city, I was beguiled and intrigued, and determined to come back and stay longer. And I did, to spend a year in Vietnam, most of it in Hanoi, to research a book about Vietnam's traditional culture, before it disappeared with the older generation.

During my stay in Hanoi, I discovered that there are a multitude of Hanois: Hanoi of the old poet and scholar; Hanoi of the bamboo pole-balancing itinerate street vendor; Hanoi of the human cog in the government apparatus; Hanoi of the tinsmith banging away in the Old Quarter of Thirty-Six Streets; Hanoi of the student grappling to conquer computer software, Western marketing and English, who ends his day sipping *bia hoi* in a pavement cafe; Hanoi of the elaborately costumed performer of traditional Vietnamese opera *(tuong);* Hanoi of the cyclo driver, fast disappearing in favour of motorbike taxis *(xe om)* and ordinary four-wheeled taxis; and now, there is the Hanoi of the aspiring executive working for a joint-venture, multinational; Hanoi of the architect, designing new office blocks and shopping centres; Hanoi of the ambitious entrepreneur, setting up new factories; and Hanoi of the investor, trading in shares in the recently established Hanoi stock exchange.

Now after nearly fifty years of wars and poverty – World War II (1940-1945), the French Indo-Chinese War (1946-1954), the Vietnam War (1965-1975), the overthrow of Pol Pot in Cambodia (1978-1989) and the more recent border skirmish with China (1979) – in Vietnam's surge forward to repair its economy and catch up with the twenty-first century, Hanoi keeps reinventing itself piecemeal, in such a rush that it can hardly wait for the tailor to finish the suit before throwing on the new jacket over the tattered shirt and rushing into the street. Rebuilding and renovation are all around. A travel agent one week becomes a cafe the next.

It would be fascinating to watch a historian-directed computer reconstruction of Hanoi's development as a city from its very beginnings.

Opening scene would have to be the old Chinese fort on the bank of the Red river (Hong Song) – China dominated the Viet people from 179BC to 938AD, despite repeated insurrections and several brief periods of freedom from Chinese rule. On gaining independence in 938, the Vietnamese Ngo dynasty set up a capital at Hoa Lu, forty-six miles (73 km) south of Hanoi and named the nation Dai Viet (Great Viet) – as in Great Britain.

The screen would then melt to a royal barge on the Red river in a steamy summer, carrying the first emperor of another new dynasty, Ly Thai To. Overwhelmed by his vision of a celestial, golden flying dragon, obviously an auspicious sign, Ly Thai To moved his capital from Hoa Lu to the Red river delta and in 1010, founded a new capital city, which naturally, had to be called the Flying Dragon (Thang Lang).

His new royal citadel (Hoang Thanh), an enormous walled square, he built on the bank of the To Lich river, a tributary running from the south-west into the Red river.

East of the citadel in the centuries to follow, the civilian or commercial district of craft guilds, now known as the Old Quarter of Thirty-Six Streets, sprang up to serve the imperial court in a triangle created by the Red river to the east, the To Lich river to the west and the Kim Nguu river across the south.

Glance at any old map of Hanoi – in feudal times the rivers and lakes of the Red river delta, scattered like shallow puddles on a lumpy surface, covered far wider areas – and it is easy to see how difficult it must have been to build a city and keep it dry on the shifting banks of a seasonal monsoon flooding river delta.

Dykes along the river banks and earthen ramparts were laboriously built to protect and surround the city from the seasonal floods and attack, the most important infrastructures of feudal Vietnam. A few centuries later, the earthen ramparts of the dykes were replaced by brick and guarded by twenty-one fortified gates into the walled city.

Skipping over several tumultuous centuries which saw the Viets repulse Kublai Khan's Mongolian hordes three times (1258, 1285 and 1288); repeated attacks on Thang Long by the Chinese – easy, just torch the wood and thatch – who the Viets repulsed again and again in the twelfth, thirteenth, fifteenth and eighteenth centuries; plus several attempts by the Chams, the Indianized kingdoms to the south, to recover their lost lands by ransacking Hanoi in the fourteenth century – skip all these conflicts or the computer screen would become a turmoil of fire and smoke and people scurrying to safety.

The poor Viet people, who became the Vietnamese, have been besieged and beleaguered by wars and military conflicts since the very stirrings of their united existence.

Finally, during the early fifteenth century under the Le dynasty, the city attained the peak of peaceful feudal development. Pagodas, temples and libraries were built and literature in *chu nom,* the old Vietnamese script using Chinese characters to express Vietnamese words, flourished. Houses began to be built of brick, often with two storeys.

Dissolve to the next major restructuring, the total destruction of the by then Le dynasty's citadel, by the usurping Nguyen dynasty, who moved the capital from Thang Long down country to Hue, after which Thang Long was demoted to being no more than a provincial capital and renamed Hanoi.

It was the second Nguyen emperor, Minh Mang, who tore down Hanoi's old feudal citadel and replaced it with a slightly smaller, citadel-fortress in the style of the French military architect, Vauban.

The next dramatic transformation came when the French seized power and in turn demolished Gia Long's Vauban-style citadel-fortress (1897), all but a flag tower, which the French retained as a watchtower and the old north gate. Today, both citadels are long gone, but for the old flag tower and the north gate. And one old city gate – the eastern gate, Quang Chuong (Dong Ha), now standing a bit inland from the Red river – are all that remain from imperial feudal times.

However, trumping the watchtower and the eastern gate in seniority are several early pagodas, devotedly restored and rebuilt over the centuries. One need not be religious to appreciate the enduring esteem the inhabitants of Hanoi hold for these precious places of worship. One goes back to the sixth century, audaciously named For the Defense of the Nation – built during a brief respite from Chinese domination, several centuries before the founding of Thang Long as the capital in 1010.

The screen would then suddenly be streaked with the straight lines of new French streets on more or less a grid system, broad, tree-lined boulevards, numerous landmark government buildings and grandiose villas popping up south of the Old Quarter in what was to become the French colonial style of South East Asia: ochre walls, mansard roofs, louvered shuttered windows and covered verandas. Add a bridge across the Red river, railway tracks running north and south, tram lines and roads out of the city in the four cardinal directions.

However, like any virtual visit of a computer restructuring, this is to rush along too quickly to appreciate the metamorphoses, or conversely, the sometimes cataclysmic events that forced the city to rebuild and re-invent itself so many times. Let me lead you on a few leisurely strolls and meanderings through Vietnam's living history and the real Hanoi that I have come to love.

First let me show you around enchanting Hoan Kiem lake, the peaceful heart of Hanoi with its fiery flamboyant blossoms, its willows drifting like green waterfalls into the still water, its stone Turtle pagoda on a tuft of an islet and its graceful red, arched bridge to an island temple, my enduring image of Hanoi. Then after a stroll round the cathedral area, we'll wander the higgledy-piggledy lanes of the Old Quarter where village craftsmen along these narrow, crowded streets have followed in their fathers' trades for generation upon generation. We'll then explore Hanoi's French colonial legacy, the oldest pagodas and the toy town *nojveau riche* towers around West Lake, as well as the new satellite suburbs.

Amongst it all, Hanoi's oldest pagodas and temples remain, tranquil in the midst of urban chaos and noise. At nightfall when families sit round their doorways sipping bowls of soup, when the taxis stop hooting, when the vroom-vroom of motorbikes dies down, when cyclo drivers stop clanging their bells and park their vehicles, only then does this restless city breathe a sigh of tranquillity.

A WALK AROUND HOAN KIEM LAKE

Where the fatherland is, there also is found the hero
– Vietnamese proverb

Whenever I wake up early in Hanoi, I slip out of my hotel and make for the Bon Mua cafe at the south-west corner of Hoan Kiem lake where I savour an aromatic, strong yet mellow cup of Vietnamese coffee. Not many French or Italians, who swear by their own coffee, realize that most of their coffee comes from Vietnam, now the second largest coffee exporter in the world after Brazil.

To linger over a coffee under the trees overlooking the lake in the early morning is to watch Hanoi awakening. Boys with footballs bounce by, old ladies in neat rows wave wooden swords in rhythm to a ghetto blaster, a man stretches his legs against one of the trees bordering the lake, a jogger lopes past and just occasionally, facing the stone Turtle Tower on an islet in the lake, an oldster moves gracefully through the poses of *tai chi*. It's all over by half past seven when offices open.

Through the years, the park surrounding the lake has been much improved, benches placed along the winding paths, paved with scallop shell-shaped tiles. But it is the old banyan trees, the drifts of delicate leaves of the flowering flamboyant, willow and tamarind trees framing any view of Hoan Kiem that make any stroll around the lake such an aesthetic pleasure.

The first of many Vietnamese legends that any visitor hears on arriving in Hanoi is the story of Le Loi (born 1384) and his magic sword – and how the lake got its name –

Having ruled Vietnam for a thousand years from 179BC to 938AD, once again in the fifteenth century, the armies of the Chinese Ming surged south and re-conquered the Viets. During this second, mercifully brief period of Chinese rule (1407-1727), the Chinese systematically eradicated local Viet culture, breaking stone stelae in temples, destroying Buddhist pagodas. Entire libraries of Buddhist works compiled over the previous four

17

centuries of independence were burnt or seized and carted off to China. The Viets found this Ming domination particularly unbearable.

According to legend, the emperor of the waters (Long Quan) decided it was high time to intervene. At that time there lived a fisherman, who one night when he lifted his net, found to his astonishment that it contained a sword.

Recognizing it as a sign, he joined the volunteers to fight against the Chinese. One day the commander-in-chief, General Le Loi, happened to stop at the fisherman's hut and noticed the splendid sword gleaming in one corner. Engraved on the metal were the words, 'By the Will of Heaven.'

A day or two later when Le Loi and his troops were forced to retreat to a forest, General Le Loi noticed something shiny at the top of a banyan tree and climbing up, found a sword hilt inlaid with jade. It was then that he remembered the strange sword in the fisherman's hut. Sensing the supernatural, he carried the hilt to the fisherman's hut and not to his surprise, found that the sword fitted perfectly.

The fisherman gladly relinquished the sword to the general and from that time on, Le Loi's troops won battle after battle, the strength of his army seemingly magnified tenfold. At long last, the Viets were liberated from the detested Ming.

Le Loi declared himself emperor and sometime later, one day while boating on the lake in the heart of the capital, suddenly the sacred golden turtle (Kim Quy) rose to the surface of the water, approached the royal boat and spoke: 'Please be so kind as to return to my master, the emperor of the kingdom of the waters, the sacred sword he entrusted to you.'

Standing in the boat, Le Loi felt the sword begin to quiver, so he threw it into the lake. The turtle dived, surfaced holding the sword in his mouth and dived again. Since that time, what had been called simply Green Water (Luc Thuy) has been known as Hoan Kiem, lake of the Restored Sword.

Historically, it was indeed General Le Loi who defeated the Ming in 1427, who took the throne and established the Le dynasty. Curiously in 1965, when the Americans were escalating the war, a giant turtle was caught in Hoan Kiem lake and its five hundred fifty-pound preserved body is still displayed as a talisman in the temple of the Jade Mountain (Ngoc Son) on the

18

island in the lake. Biologists estimate that the turtle was approximately five hundred years old, its birth neatly coinciding with the fifteenth century legend of Le Loi.

A word about kings and emperors. Normally the Vietnamese refer to their rulers as kings, pointing out that their 'empire' only extended over the Cham kingdoms in the south. However, as Vietnamese rulers exercised absolute power over their subjects to a degree that European kings might well have envied, the Western mind tends to think of them as oriental emperors.

SOUTH BANK OF THE LAKE

From Bon Mua cafe I make my way along the south bank of the lake through the park, opposite the lacquer shops as they are starting to open. At the south-east corner of the lake at the junction of Dinh Tien Huang and Dinh Le Streets, the multi-storey Trang Tam shopping centre boasted Hanoi's first escalator a few years ago when it opened. Ironically, it stands on the corner once occupied by an exclusive French department store, Goddard's, which in turn was built where the Lady Kieu (Ba Kieu) temple, sometimes called Thien Tien or Chan Tien (Heavenly or Genuine Immortals) temple, once stood. The temple, built in the reign of Emperor Le Thanh Tong (1619-1628), was dedicated to the goddess, Lieu Hanh.

The French had little or no respect for pagodas and temples. If they wanted a site, whatever was there was demolished.

Approaching pagodas and temples in Vietnam, the foreigner can take two views: simply to admire the beauty of the architecture in its setting, the intricate carving and rich lacquer, the sculpture and the paintings, purely as the work of skilled artists and artisans or, by attempting to unravel who the various statues represent, the symbolism of the paintings and what the parallel sentences in Chinese ideograms mean. Taking the latter approach, you get different explanations from guides, monks, scholars and even written works of history. It's not unlike trying to fight your way through a thicket of Catholic saints, only to discover that each country has its own set of saints. Just when you think you are beginning to get a handle on Vietnamese deities and religious personages, you discover that the same deity has half a dozen incarnations – then multiply that by Animism,

19

Taoism, Confucianism and Buddhism. As each religion came along, the accommodating Vietnamese have taken whatever deities they needed and spliced them on to those they already had.

But faced with a pagoda or a temple, full to brimming with life-sized gilt personages staring back, it is all too easy to let curiosity leap out of control and try to find out who each and every one of them is, or was.

EAST BANK OF THE LAKE

Turning left along the boulevard bordering the eastern shore of the lake, the Emperor Dinh Tien Huang well deserved a major street in the heart of Vietnam's capital city named after him. It was he, who on the death of the first emperor of independent Vietnam in 944, rallied, negotiated and cajoled the rivalling factions known as the twelve warlords, to accept unification of the state, which he as emperor renamed Dai Co Viet (again, Great Viet, or maybe Very Great Viet).

On the subject of names, may I suggest in the interest of sanity that you do not try to remember the numerous infernally similar Vietnamese names or the chronology of Vietnam's extraordinarily convoluted history. Just enjoy the stories and at the risk of repetition, you will be reminded of who they were as we go along. For those who prefer a framework on which to hang it, there is a historic appendix listing the dynasties. Note, it is the first of a Vietnamese emperor's three names that designates the dynasty – or the family or clan name of a contemporary Vietnamese.

Vietnamese pronunciation, incidentally, is fraught with the uncertainties of a tonal language. Each one-syllable word can be pronounced six different ways (tones) in the North, five different ways (tones) in the South – and as a result has five or six different meanings – at least. So when searching for an address, it is foolhardy not to show the printed words to a Vietnamese.

One street further up Dinh Tien Huang at the corner of Dinh Le, is what I think of as the jewellery mart, a vast ground-floor space holding a conglomeration of small, presumably competing jewellery stalls, a bit like a department store. Well worth browsing. Opposite the jewellery mart is what looks like a rather boring example of modernity. A two-storey circular portico, supported by smooth pillars, shelters the corner entrance. In fact, this is a late French colonial building, the Domestic Post Office, designed by Henri Cerutti and completed in 1942.

Next door, facing the lake is the even more modern International Post Office, built in the sixties. The original, rather more elegant French colonial post office, its mansard roof and small oriole windows, designed by Auguste-Henri Vildieu, is located at the corner of Dinh Tien Hoang Street and Le Thach Street further along.

The site occupied by the jewellery mart and the post offices has quite a chequered history. During the latter part of the Le Dynasty (1545-1788), when in actuality the Trinh clan exercised power over the weak Le emperor, a Trinh mansion known as the Five Dragons pavilion (Ngu Long) stood on this spot, where the Trinh lord used to relax on hot summer days. At the time it must have been rather audacious for even a Trinh lord to decorate his pavilion with five dragons as in Vietnam, the dragon is the dual symbol of the emperor and power. Much later, when the Nguyen dynasty of Hue seized the throne (1802), the Five Dragons pavilion, in fact, all Trinh mansions – rivals of the Nguyen clan for centuries – were destroyed.

On the foundations of the pavilion, a devoted Buddhist mandarin, Nguyen Dong Giai (then governor of Hanoi), raised funds and built a pagoda in the 1840s.

The new pagoda, as is so often the case in Vietnam, was variously called Bao An (Debt of Gratitude to One's Parents), though the people nicknamed it Quan Thuong (High-Ranking Mandarin's pagoda) and Lien Tri (Lotus Pond). So attractive was this pagoda under fruit and frangipani trees, surrounded by lotus carpeted moats, its walls elaborately carved with scenes from hell, that it became very popular with people of several faiths – there was even a folk song extolling its beauty.

Along come the French in 1892, building roads where no roads had been before, running roughshod over Hanoi, demolishing pagodas and temples, razing whole sections of the city – south of Hoan Kiem Lake – in order to impose their plans for a new colonial administrative capital. The beautiful Bao An/Quan Thuong/Lien Tri pagoda, which spread over an extensive area, was demolished in favour of their new post office

21

and the *Palais du Gouvernement Général,* behind it. A new road separated the temple site from its square brick gate, evokably named, the Favourable Winds (Hoa Phong). The gate is now all that remains of Bao An, standing rather forlornly in the park beside the lake opposite, its yawning entrances, indeed, open to the four winds.

Strolling on northward, the long narrow green park on the right has had an equally complicated history. According to an 1831 map, it was the site of Tien Quan fort of the northern governor – at the time when Hanoi was demoted by the Nguyen dynasty to being no more than a provincial capital.

Before that, there had been a lake nearby, prosaically called Elephant lake, where elephants from the royal stables were bathed. Arrive the French, who decided it would make an excellent park, the first they built in Hanoi. In it they placed a small version of New York's Statue of Liberty, which must have been galling to the Vietnamese, living under colonial rule. The Vietnamese called her Dam Yoi (Western lady in flowing dress). A little later in 1890, the French installed a statue of Paul Bert, the first civilian French Governor General to Annam and Tonkin and changed the name of the park to Paul Bert Square. Paul Bert had begun his term in 1886 – the Indo-Chinese Federation was declared in 1887 – and died before completing his term.

The statue of Paul Bert, holding a flag in his left hand, his right hand held patronizing over the head of the Vietnamese governor of the North, Nguyen Trong Hop, must also have rankled the Vietnamese.

As the story goes, for a time the statues of Dam Yoi and Paul Bert stood side by side. Then the statue of Paul Bert disappeared to await shipment of a marble base. When Dam Yoi was eventually moved to Cua Nam, local wags joked: 'Paul Bert married Dam Yoi, but Dam Yoi had an affair while Mr Bert was away, so when a servant told Mr Bert about the affair, he chased Dam Yoi with a stick to Cua Nam.'

Eventually, the French built a music pavilion (Nha Ken) in the park where a band played on Sunday afternoons. To the locals, it became known as the trumpet house.

Ever ironic in their wit, when the French later erected a statue of the French philosopher, Ernest Renan (1823-1892), facing the then newly built *Banque d'Indochine* (now the Central Bank of

Vietnam), the local people joshed: 'The ears of this progressive idealist have to listen to the jingle of coins from the bank as well as to the music from the bandstand.' Both statues disappeared with the arrival of the Japanese in 1945. For a time, the bandstand became an aviary.

In 1954, following the defeat of the French at Dien Bien Phu, the park was renamed Chi Linh after a guerrilla base used by General Le Loi, he of the magic sword, who defeated the Chinese. In 1985, the park took the name of the Indian prime minister, Indira Gandhi, who had befriended Vietnam at a time when the country had few friends.

The park has recently changed names yet again, very appropriately to honour Ly Thai To, the emperor in the boat on the Red river, who saw the flying dragon and founded the capital, Thang Long. At long last, his capital city has paid him due homage. Three marble paved courtyards guarded by stone railings embellished with stone lotus buds rise to where the majestic bronze statue of the emperor, wearing flowing court robes and holding the scroll containing the edict that decreed the founding of the city, stands mounted high on a plinth.

In a compromise between modernity and tradition and possibly political correctness, the steps approaching the upper level are flanked by banisters decorated with clouds and waves; in a royal palace or tomb temple, it would have been dragons denoting royalty.

Ly Thai To's origins are interesting, illustrating how through the centuries there has been a certain social mobility in Vietnamese society, either through scholarship or the military. Ly Thai To (974-1028) was born a fatherless child in Bac Ninh Province. When he was three years old, he was adopted and given the family name, Ly. While he was very young, Ly Cong Uan was taught by a monk; when he grew up, he studied military strategy.

When the Emperor Le Ngoa Trieu died in 1009, Ly Cong Uan, by then thirty-five years old and general commander-in-chief, took the throne, founding the Ly dynasty that lasted for two hundred sixteen years through nine kings. His name during his reign became Thuan Thien (Pursuant to God's Will); his posthumous name, Ly Thai To (Ancient Patriarch). Considering the implications of name changes in the past, I hope that the park never again has to change its name. The delightful, hexagonal

23

bandstand pavilion with its double-tiled roof, tucked behind Ly Thai To's statue, has now reverted to its original function.

To make a very quick detour – through the park to the far right corner, the park touches a boulevard named after one of Vietnam's most illustrious military heroes, Ngo Quyen the liberator, the first emperor of independent Vietnam. The Vietnamese are justifiably proud of this distant general's military acumen over the Han Chinese. How the Vietnamese triumphed over the Chinese demonstrates the cunning strategy the Vietnamese have always had to employ in order to defeat far more powerful foes throughout the centuries.

In the case of Ngo Quyen, he had the intelligence to listen to the advice of an old woman who lived on the bank of the Bach Dong river near Haiphong. Accordingly, he arranged a series of spikes in the riverbed that were covered at high tide. The Vietnamese in their tiny thatch-roofed sampans then lured the Chinese galleons to follow them up river. When the tide turned, the Chinese junks became impaled on the spikes. The Vietnamese set fire to the Chinese junks, forcing them to flee and fight on shore. With this momentous victory in 938, General Ngo Quyen ended a thousand years of hateful Chinese domination – the Viets were free and independent at last. Ngo Quyen proclaimed himself emperor and set up his capital in Co Loa, forty-six miles (73 km) south of Hanoi. The battle is touchingly depicted in a model in the History Museum.

Sure enough, well within coin-jingling distance of the music pavilion, the former *Banque d'Indochine,* now the Central Bank of Vietnam, stands as heavy as a safe in its art deco grandeur, across the junction of Ngo Quyen and Ly Thai To – this latter grand boulevard renamed to commemorate the imperial founder of the city.

Just around the corner to the right, the former *Palais du Gouvernement Général* now flies the red flag emblazoned with the gold star of the Democratic Republic of Vietnam and serves as the government guest house for visiting dignitaries. A central staircase and ramps from each side sweep up to the grand entrance, curling wrought iron decorating its peaked canopy.

The grounds of Bao An pagoda must have been quite extensive to have taken in the park and the areas occupied by both the bank and the *Palais du Gouvernement.*

24

Returning to the lake along Le Lai on the north side of the park, a green-shuttered, two-storey white building with a corner entrance strikes a remarkable resemblance to old photographs of the fashionable social club and casino of the French, *le Club Sportif,* minus the wide, raised terrace in the photograph. At the corner of Le Lai and Dinh Tieng Hoang stands the old French *Mairie,* the mayor's office.

Continuing north up Dinh Tien Hoang beside the lake, the modern white landmark building on the right houses the Hanoi People's Central Committee, a monumental assemblage of heavy, vertical marble rectangles, its weighty canopied entrance softened somewhat by formal topiary-trimmed, potted bonsai trees. It is built on the site of the former Duong Vo temple (1757), dedicated to three master trainers of the elephant corps. The French originally nabbed this temple site for their *Hôtel de Ville.* Now the Vietnamese have built their own stately monument.

A little further along Dinh Tien Huang, the modern Monument to the Martyrs of the August Revolution arrests your attention. Designed by sculptor Nguyen Kim Giao, the enormous sculpture represents three figures: a woman holding a sword and two soldiers, one kneeling with a gun. The tribute at the base translates: 'We are determined to devote our lives to the life of the fatherland,' a common sentiment during the French Indo-China War at a time when a group of 'life-and-death commandos' (Cam Tu Quan) had been established to undertake particularly perilous, sometimes suicidal missions such as attacking French tanks with small bombs.

Immediately behind this monument is what remains of Ba Kieu temple, buttoned up and locked except for the first and fifteenth of each lunar month. It is thought that the founder was Chua Trinh, wife of the first scribe, a high-ranking mandarin to a late seventeenth century Le emperor. It is dedicated to Vietnam's mother goddess, Lieu Hanh, who is worshipped as the goddess of fertility and abundance. Inside, beside her are the mothers of the forest and the sea and a newish statue of Quan Am, Vietnam's goddess of mercy, she of a thousand arms and eyes, who protects men from storms, fires and demons and grants fertility to women.

Just opposite the little temple, a graceful, red-arched bridge leads to the lake temple of the Jade Mountain (Ngoc Son). The Huc bridge (The pronounced Tay) has been variously translated as – 'to keep the morning bright, perch of the morning sun, the rainbow, the rising sun and the sun's ladder,' because like the sun, the bridge arcs from east to west. I rather prefer the image of the sun perching on the curved red bridge. Picturesque The Huc bridge only dates from 1925; originally, the bridge was bamboo.

As you might well imagine, this ultra-prime site, Jade Island, has a colourful history. Once no more than a wild hillock of an island, Emperor Le Thanh Tong (1460-1497) built a small pavilion on it and on the fifteenth of every lunar month and at full moon, he and his entourage would come to the island to drink wine, write poems and fish. How very civilized.

At the end of the sixteenth century, a powerful Trinh lord – the same Trinh clan who built the Five Dragons pavilion – used to watch naval manoeuvres from here. At that time, Hoan Kiem lake was much larger and linked to the Red river. It is still linked by an underground channel. Later, during Lord Trinh Giang's 'reign', he built a large pleasure palace (Khan Thuy, 1739) on the island for fishing and drinking parties. When the late Le emperor, Le Chieu Thong, came to power – as was the practice in those days, to obliterate as much as possible of the previous regime – he burnt not only Khanh Thuy palace, but all of the buildings related to the Trinh clan.

Splendidly carved Ngoc Son temple is actually fairly recent, built towards the end of the nineteenth century when a devoted Buddhist, Tin Trai, collected donations from nearby residents to build it. Ngoc Son originally had a bell tower, destroyed in 1843. The pagoda subsequently became a Taoist temple honouring three deities: the god of literature (Van Xuong), the god of medicine (La To) and Quan Cong, a Chinese general of the third century known for his courage and straight forwardness. When a contract was signed, people came before Quan Cong to 'seal the deal' – a promise made before him was binding.

What to a Westerner might look like rather whimsically painted nursery animals on the gates turn out to be deeply serious Taoist symbols. The yellow prancing horse-dragon carries eight *i ching,* representing the symbols for the eight elements on his back. The turtle, carrying a book and a sword, indicates that military might and knowledge must go together. The 'flirty' tiger with long eyelashes and the truncated dragon, who seems to have deposited bits of his anatomy amongst the clouds, are Taoist symbols of – stability. The carp are gazing at the moon's reflection and the pine tree of roosting storks, longevity.

A tower to the left of the bridge (Thap But), said to be in the shape of a paint brush, was built by the poet, Nguyen Van Sieu – an extremely thick, tiered stone paintbrush, the brush is on top. It symbolizes literacy, education and scholars. On his paint brush tower in *chu nom* calligraphy, Nguyen Van Sieu inscribed the words, 'painting on the blue sky.' Understandably, the French dubbed Ngoc Son the 'literary temple' and for a time, 'borrowed' it for concerts before building a concert hall, now the Thang Long Water Puppet Theatre, a few steps north along Dinh Tien Hoang.

Fighting the midges, I walk round the back of the temple (the wrong way, anti-clockwise), past the rock garden in a pond and eventually, rediscover the highly varnished turtle, a soft-backed *rafetus leloii,* glaring beadily from inside his glass case (in a room to the left of the temple entrances.)

A brazier in the courtyard to the left of the temple gives off the fumes of burning paper – pretend money to bring prosperity, or burnt messages being carried by the smoke to one's ancestors. The Wave-Stopping Pavilion (Tran Ba), beside the lake, was originally the entrance to the temple when it was reached by boat. The name, Wave-Stopping Pavilion, conjures up watery images, but no, it was built in the nineteenth century as a symbol of resistance to 'waves of foreign influence.' Sheltered by a weeping fig tree, elderly men sit playing Vietnamese chess *(co tuong)* – or composing poetry. Bonsai trees form elegant silhouettes against the lake. Indeed, a heavenly spot on a hot summer afternoon.

Inside the temple, two giant gilt parrots guard the first altar. The story goes that the parrots attached themselves to a woman who had done some wrong – a gossip, or perhaps she had told lies – repeating everything she said to ensure that she told the truth. Up three steps, the second temple is dedicated to the warrior figure, Quang Cong, the Chinese general of the Thuc Han dynasty, celebrated for his valour and loyalty. There is some discussion as to whether the life-sized red lacquer horse is his stead or the horse in Tao mythology that carried the Book of Changes over the Huang Ha river. Symbols can sometimes become infernally intertwined.

Also honoured is La To, father of traditional medicine and one of eight Taoist deities who sought the elixir of long life. The statue in the topmost position represents Van Xuong, the literary scholar responsible for doctoral examinations.

The third temple room holds a golden robed figure under a richly carved filigree canopy, the famous general, Tran Hung Dao. One of Vietnam's most revered military heroes, it was Tran Hung Dao who defeated the Mongols three times in the thirteenth century and he is fittingly commemorated by countless streets named after him throughout Vietnam.

Beside the altar are 'votive weapons' mounted on pikes: 'symbols of power.' An elegant pair of bronze, arch-necked cranes, symbol of longevity and endurance, serve as the celestial transport for good souls to heaven.

The temple dedicated to General Tran Hung Dao was added by none other than Ho Chi Minh himself, who felt that Ngoc Son Temple should honour a Vietnamese rather than a Chinese general. An understandable sentiment, particularly in this most prominent position. After all, Vietnam is hardly short of military heroes and Ngoc Son is doubtless Hanoi's most popular temple, probably second only to Ho Chi Minh's Mausoleum as Hanoi's most visited tourist attraction. All manner of souvenirs are on sale in its shops (plural).

Vietnamese visitors far outnumber foreign tourists. The hopeful public photographers – the Vietnamese like to record their visit to a famous landmark to show the folks back home – and the strolling vendors selling tiny wooden cheeping birds, postcards and paperback guidebooks, can become a bit much around the temple these days. Continuing north round the lake I overhear a woman saying, 'We've been buying and buying and buying. There comes a moment when you've done buying.'

NORTH END OF THE LAKE

Skirting along the north shore of Hoan Kiem, buses now stop at what was formerly the French tram station. Quite by chance, in my hotel I meet a man, returning after an absence of fifty years, who remembered riding the trams as a child. Earlier in the nineteenth century, this area held a coconut grove called Van Dua, used by the Vietnamese and later the French – as an execution grounds for organisers of revolts.

The open space where five roads meet with a newish fountain in the centre is ponderously named – Progressive Eastern School for Justice Square (Dong Kinh Nghia Thuc). In 1946, a fierce battle took place here. Vietnamese soldiers armed with no more than grenades and Molotov cocktails pitted themselves against French tanks. Learning this, the Monument to the Martyrs of the August Revolution nearby, takes on new meaning. The square is now dominated by Kentucky Fried Chicken.

Thuy Ta (Lake Pavilion) cafe, just south of Kinh Nghia Thuc Square, its terrace overhanging the lake, is a delightful spot to linger over a lemonade or a bowl of ice cream. Built by the French just before the outbreak of World War II, it takes little imagination to envision it in the moonlight as a fashionable, romantic dance hall during the last days of French Indo-China. The earlier cafe that had occupied the spot, run by a mandarin's daughter named Miss Thuoc, had previously attracted a clientele of young intellectuals.

WESTERN BANK OF THE LAKE

Turning south along the west side of the lake, we find ourselves in Le Thai To Street, not to be confused with Ly Thai To, the founder of Hanoi. This Le Thai To was the dynastic name of General Le Loi (1385-1433), who freed the Vietnamese from Ming Chinese domination (1428) with the aid of the sacred sword. Seemingly just to confuse hapless foreigners, every monarch took a new name when he mounted the throne and another posthumous name when he died.

During the French colonial era, number 8 Le Thai To marked the front gate of the villa of a French official named Morche, whose vast garden extended to the lane behind, Hang Hanh. He was eventually imprisoned by the Japanese. Later, during the Indo-Chinese War in 1945 and 1946, Ho Chi Minh spent several nights in his villa, shuttling back and forth between the villa and the former French *Palais du Gouvernement* on Ngo Quyen to avoid arrest. The sleek offices of a Vietnamese finance and insurance company have replaced the villa, but a plaque commemorates the historic site. Just a few steps further along, I had been using an ATM at ANZ Bank long before I discovered the stories of the building's origin. Number 14 Le Thai To had served as the headquarters of the French Military Commander of the North (from August 1946). On the night of 19 December 1946, Vietnamese resistance fighters attacked the residence of the French general, Morliere. But as the attackers entered the gate, their weapons jammed, allowing Morliere time to leap into a jeep to try to escape. The Vietnamese soldiers frantically threw grenades after him and the fifth one exploded, setting the jeep alight and wounding the officer sitting next to Morliere. One wonders how different history might have been if Morliere had been killed that night, for it was French troops under his command who were ordered to occupy Haiphong, marking the official beginning of the French Indo-Chinese War.

During the Vietnam War, the building became a rest and recreation centre for Vietnamese communist soldiers from the South. Later, it was used by the Association for the Preservation of National Culture. ANZ Bank and *The People (Nhan Dan)* newspaper offices now share the property.

According to legend, in the middle of the Le Dynasty (1428-1527), the power-behind-the-throne Trinh lords built a sprawling palace complex along this west bank of the lake (and another along the east bank). The villages on either side were known as the right and left villages. I am indebted to Vietnamese writer and scholar, Huu Ngoc, for a description written by Le Huu Trac (1720-1791), considered to be one of the fathers of traditional medicine in Viet Nam, who wrote under the charming, self-deprecating pen name, Old Lazy Bones (Lan Ong). The doctor wrote not only a description of his professional visit to a Trinh palace to treat a sickly young prince, but he was so impressed that he wrote a poem as well to express his delight and wonder at what he had seen. Of course, we don't know which Trinh palace.

'When we arrived at the rear entrance to the palace, the mandarin who had summoned me acted as my guide. We passed through two gates in succession and took an alley to the left. I raised my eyes to take a look at the trees and shrubs. All around, birds were chirping. Rare flowers were blooming and heavenly scents were wafted by the wind. Criss-crossed balusters lined the verandas. Messengers carrying orders shuffled back and forth. At each gate, guards controlled people's comings and goings, demanding presentation of (stone) tablets, serving as guarantees of safe-conduct.

'I was eventually allowed to enter (the palace). We followed a veranda in the west and came to a large building on both sides of which royal palanquins painted red and gold stood in attendance. In the middle on a platform was a gilded royal bed with a pink hammock hanging over it. In front of the bed and on each side were tables laid with uncommon objects. I cast a furtive glance at them and moved with my head bowed. We passed through a door and arrived at a large, tall building whose beams and pillars were painted red and gold. I whispered a question to the mandarin who had summoned me. Here is his answer.

'We just passed through the Great Palace named Picking up the Coniza (sic). The building with a second storey is called the Crimson Palace and is reserved for the crown prince, who is in the habit of drinking tea there, hence its nickname, the Tea Room. In fact, it is the Medicine Room, but because people are shy of uttering this word, they prefer to call it the Tea Room.'

'After the meal a eunuch went running to invite the Great Chancellor to come in. The Great Chancellor for fear that I might get lost, ordered me to follow him in his steps. When we arrived at the set place, he pushed aside the brocade hangings and we entered. Inside, it was dark and I could not make out any door or other opening.

'Hangings succeeded hangings, each preceded by a lit candle which allowed one to see one's way. After four or five sets of tapestries, we came to a room in the middle of which stood a gold-bedecked bed. On the bed sat the little prince, a child of five or six years old, clad in red silk. A large candle was planted on a bronze stand, giving out some light. Close to the bed was a dragon-sculpted royal armchair, lacquered red with gold ornaments and a brocade cushion. Behind a silk hanging embroidered with gold and silver thread, a group of palace maids were huddled together. I vaguely saw their painted faces and pink garments. The room smelled of flowers and incense. I surmised that his highness had just left the armchair and retired behind a tapestry, so that I could feel at ease when taking the pulse of his little son.'

Here is the poem the doctor wrote as a memoir of the occasion.

Guards carrying golden spears stand at the thousand gates
Under the southern skies, this is the most respected place
Multi-storey painted palaces and buildings rise towards
the sky
Pearl blinds and jade balusters shine under the rising sun
Flowers continuously emit delicate scents
In the royal gardens the voices of parrots are heard
To the commoner that I am, these enchanting places
have so far been unknown.
I remain speechless, like a fisherman
straying to peach blossom stream.
(tr Huu Ngoc)

An insight concerning euphemisms, at which I suspect the exceedingly civil Vietnamese still excel. In polite company, especially at court, certain words such as 'medicine' and 'death' were never uttered. It is said that new wives arriving at the latter Nguyen court were sometimes so afraid of uttering such a word by accident that they remained completely silent for a year!

Next door to ANZ Bank at number 16, a statue mounted on a tall pillar depicts General Le Loi, alias Emperor Le Thai To, holding the magic sword, erected in 1896. Tucked behind Le Thai To's statue is the Nam Huong temple, (entrance from the street behind, Hang Trong). It is dedicated to the gods of the four compass directions, but when it attained the status of a certified historical site in 1995, it was renamed the Le King temple.

IN THE CATHEDRAL QUARTER

New spirits fear old ones
– Vietnamese proverb

Detouring a bit from the lake, from Le Thai To Street along the west bank, we take a sharp right into Drum Street (Hang Thong). Several centuries ago Hang Thong formed part of the dyke when Hoan Kiem lake lay outside the dyke, before the course of the Red river shifted to the east. In those days the street was made up of several tiny villages known as the Five Guilds Area of Seven Crafts. Inhabitants made canopies, parasols, wood blocks, wood block prints and embroidery, as well as drums. There was even a folk song that ran: 'Rich and generous people go through Wood-Turner Place.' It is still a street of colourful artisan shops selling lacquer, silk and embroidered linens.

The elaborately decorated building at the V of the sharp corner, 79 Hang Trong, has all the architectural hallmarks of the French architect, Ernest Hebrard: Buddhist swastikas are incorporated in the *bas reliefs* between the pilasters that frame the green shuttered windows, oriental style window frames and more Asian motifs lining the cornices (more of Hebrard later).

During the French colonial era, this was the headquarters of the rather pompously named Association for the Intellectual and Moral Training of the Vietnamese *(Association pour la formation intellectuel et morales des Annamites)*. That must have gone down a treat with the Vietnamese who, made to study in French, understood full well exactly what it meant. However, it was members of this scholarly literary organization who refined and compiled a Vietnamese dictionary in *quoc ngu* Romanised script.

The Viets had no written language when the Chinese first conquered them in 179 BC. Up to the early twentieth century, although Vietnamese and Chinese were completely different languages having no more than tonality in common, Chinese characters, *chu nom,* were adopted to express Vietnamese words in literature, government and legal documents. Although many Chinese words have found their way into Vietnamese – it is estimated that perhaps fifty percent of today's Vietnamese vocabulary is based on Chinese words – they have been 'Vietnamised', words meaning the same thing but pronounced quite differently.

It was midway down country that the first Christian missionaries set foot on Vietnamese soil in 1614 in the persons of an Italian Jesuit priest, Francesco Buzomi and the Portuguese priest, Diego Carvalho. A few years later, the Italian priest, Christoforo Borri, lived in and around Hoi An from 1618 to 1621. Having been thrown out of Japan following the introduction of Japan's Closed Door Policy, the Jesuit priests fled to Hoi An in central Vietnam – where Christianity was first introduced to the Vietnamese.

The Jacques-come-lately French priest, Alexandre de Rhodes, is much lauded by the French for having published the first Vietnamese dictionary in the Latin-based, Romanised *quoc ngu* script in 1651. However, according to scholars, who as proof point to the very un-French accents used in modern Vietnamese, it was these Italian and Portuguese priests who actually developed the diacritical markings system of the Romanised *quoc ngu* to enable the scriptures to be read in Vietnamese by the common people. Until then, *chu nom* ideograms could only be read by scholars.

In *quoc ngu,* the diacritical markings, accents above and beneath the vowels indicate whether they are long or short, open or closed, in the high or low registers of the six tones in the North, five tones in the South.

Having been originally devised by Catholic priests, for three hundred years *quoc ngu* was used almost exclusively by the Catholics. In the latter half of the nineteenth century, two Vietnamese Catholics, Paulus Cua and Trung Vin Ky, updated *quoc ngu* in order to translate Western works of literature and philosophy. *Quoc ngu* was declared the official language by the French in 1910 – much easier to read than the Chinese characters of *chu nom.*

Number 79 Hang Trong had further political significance. This building served as the headquarters of the National Assembly Standing Committee of Ho Chi Minh's Provisional Government, which elected members to attend the first National Assembly at the opera house, January 6, 1946. These days, it hosts a troupe of water puppets.

A little further along the street is a hidden temple built to commemorate a murder victim. Entered through a very narrow passageway, Dong Huong temple at 82 Hang Trong, is dedicated to a singer. One version of the story tells how the beautiful, talented singer was the concubine of one of the Trinh lords, who invited guests to hear her sing. It is said that the Trinh lord's wife became so jealous that she forced the singer to drink alcohol until she fell comatose, and then buried her alive – on the spot. The Trinh lord was so grieved that he had a door constructed into her coffin so that she could be given powerful antidotes to restore her to life. It is also said that she haunted the murderous wife.

Another version of the story lauds the singer for being so generous with the fortune she made singing, supporting orphans and the poor when they fell sick. This narrow temple is said to have been built directly over her tomb.

At the back of the passage, an unpromising bare room holds nothing more than a long table, chairs and a white bust of Ho Chi Minh. Then I notice a flight of stairs in the courtyard leading up to what looks like possibly a temple.

Upstairs, a couple of middle-aged women rouse themselves from a mat on the floor to greet me and one leads me by the arm inside. Above the altar in a row are what I assume to be three Trinh lords and four ladies, the altar surrounded by surprisingly ornate gilt carving to find in such a tiny temple, but then, this would have been a temple built by a wealthy and powerful Trinh lord for his favourite singer.

As I am examining the statues, my hostess is patting the back of my cotton jacket and more alarmingly – my bottom. Fortunately, I can't understand her comments, so I am uncertain as to whether she is admiring its full roundedness or exclaiming over there being so much of it. Happily, she too, is rather well rounded, so for once I don't feel like a bloated Westerner. The walls are painted with a dragon, a line of musicians and a seated lady, presumably the singer to whom the temple is dedicated.

The woman leads me along a passageway to the front of the building to another small temple containing two huge blue and white jars and a statue of the singer. The woman points to a silk cradle, which adds a bit of mystery to the plot. I give my hostess a small offering and depart. Later, a Buddhist friend explains: 'the national queen mother and her entourage.'

Leading off Hang Trong, Nha Tho Street to the left is a street of pleasant European-style restaurants. Tucked away on the left at number 3 is a tranquil, very old pagoda called the Stone Lady (Ba Da) that dates back to Le Thanh Tong's reign (1460-1497). While building new walls for the citadel in Bao Tien Tu Thap village, which then occupied a street nearby, a stone was dug up that the villagers thought resembled a woman. Not unnaturally, they thought she must be the mother goddess of the earth. At first, only a small shrine was built, but with time and the accretion of reverence, the people built a pagoda. Unfortunately, after a fire in the early 1900s, the statue disappeared and the temple became the Linh Quang Tu (Sacred Light) pagoda.

These days the large courtyard is usefully employed to park motorbikes. The doors to the pagoda are closed, but a man dozing over a table of Buddhist tracts motions me to go round the back of the pagoda, past a crowd of hanging pots of orchids, so the pagoda is still in use – someone is looking after the orchids.

The temple at the back of the pagoda holds statues of two former monks of this pagoda and a somewhat odd crowned figure wearing a glittering red head drape.

Continuing round the back of the pagoda, on the far side I find a single open doorway and go in. The dim light reveals a huge altar crowded with statues.

In front, two elaborately crowned gilt statues stand side by side, each holding a book and a water vessel, *bodhisattvas* – Buddhas who have reached enlightenment, nirvana, but who chose to remain in this world to help others in their religious quest. One holds a vessel representing benevolence – water to nurture those who have been tortured; the other holds a book, symbolizing knowledge.

Behind and above them are seated two huge gilt Buddhas, one overlooking the other, the first holding a lotus bud. *Arhats,* monks who have not yet reached nirvana, in teams of five line the walls beside a king of hell, wearing a mortarboard like a graduate, one king of hell on each side of the kneeling platform in front of the altar.

Throughout my visit I hear creaking, as though someone were creeping about. As I am leaving via the way I have come, round the back of the pagoda, I catch a glimpse of a silent young monk as he disappears into a cell. So I was being watched.

36

The pagoda may not look very old – it has been rebuilt many times. The bells and gong are fairly recent, dating from 1823, 1842 and 1881. However, attesting to its age, outside a poem on a brass plaque translates as:

Linh Quang is in the heart of Thang Long,
The way of truth is both visible and invisible,
The magic of the stone was sent from heaven to earth,
This majestic place stands near beautiful Sword Lake.

At the end of Nha Tho Street, St. Joseph's cathedral stands on the site of the former Bao Thien (Gratitude to Heaven) pagoda, one of Hanoi's oldest and most venerated places of worship, first built in 1057. A year after it was built, a twelve-storey bell tower, ten *trung* high (approx 55 ft, 18 m) was added – the tallest structure in eleventh century Thang Long. The pagoda was named Sung Khanh, the bell tower Bao Thien, both known collectively as Bao Thien. Along with the dykes, the tower was considered to be one of the most ambitious building projects of the period. A storm in 1258 toppled the upper part of the tower and in 1322, lightening destroyed the two top storeys. Then in 1426, during the Ming domination (1414-1427), the entire tower was destroyed and the bronze used for weapons. Later in the Le period, the foundations of the tower became an execution ground.

A mandarin in 1791, Pham Dinh Ho, recorded the story of the tower in Tang Thuong Ngau Luc: 'The foundation had four gates, each of which had two stone guardian deities (Kim Cuong). Every tile were engraved with the words: "Made in the fourth year of Long Thuy Thai Dinh," that is, the third year of the reign of the Ly dynasty' (1057).

Bao Thien pagoda was still standing in 1883. In 1873, the French had captured the citadel for the first time. The priest, Puginier, settled himself in nearby Nha Chung village, still the name of the street that runs in front of the cathedral. He built a small wood and thatch church, later the Chapelle des Martyrs at number 31, long since gone. There was also a small fortress nearby. In 1883, Vietnamese resistance fighters from the Tho Xuong district joined Luu Vinh Phuc's Black Flags (more of them later) to attack the church. Ironically, the priests and French soldiers took refuge around the corner in Ba Da pagoda. Sadly, all that's left of Bao Thien tower and pagoda is a bell bearing one engraved character, Long from Thang Long.

In 1884, in what must have been one of the most enraging decisions ever taken by the French to the Vietnamese, the French forced the governing mandarin of Hanoi to hand over Bao Thien pagoda in order to build their cathedral where it stood. The opening service of the yet to be completed Gothic Revival style cathedral took place on Christmas Eve of 1886. The stained glass windows were added in 1906.

These days, come Sunday, the church is so crowded with Vietnamese Catholics that they overflow into the courtyard where they stand, listening to the sermon amplified over a loud speaker. At Christmas, a creche is installed beside the entrance.

In Au Trieu Street, running alongside the cathedral, La Place is a cosy restaurant and cafe, a pleasant place to rest the feet, have a coffee, read newspapers or magazines – or have a meal – overlooking the cathedral through the trees from the terrace upstairs.

Detouring for a moment north along Ly Quoc Su Street, the Ly Quoc Su pagoda at number 50, has a curious story. A stele inside tells why the temple happened to be built in 1131.

'This temple is dedicated to Minh Khong, the national monk. Emperor Ly Than Tong caught a disease by which he seemed to turn into a tiger. Monk Minh Khong (born Nguyen Chi Thanh) cured the king and was awarded the title of National Physician (Quoc Su). The emperor also set up a purified building for the monk, which later became Ly Quoc Su temple.'

Ly Quoc Su was last restored in 1953. Once inside the gate, the carved doors of the temple are closed, but a monk wearing brown trousers and tunic – no more robes? – motions me to enter a door to one side. Removing my shoes, I find myself in a huge altar room. A pair of thick stone pillars, carved with parallel sentences in ideograms *(chu nom)* and three pairs of orange gilt columns support the large hall of worship.

Fine life-sized, red and orange lacquered statues of *arhats* line the side walls. A dazzling gilt altar to Sakyamuni, a statue of Buddha as a baby, occupies the central position. An eight-armed Buddha stands behind it at the feet of a large seated Buddha, flanked by two crowned *bodihisattvas,* Buddhas who have attained nirvana but choose to remain in this world to help others in their religious quest. In the highest place of honour, a crowned figure draped in yellow silk represents the revered monk, Minh Khong. The stone statues either side of him are said to date from the Le era (17th C).

It is not until I am leaving the temple that I notice the three huge Buddhas of past, present and future seated high on a canopy above the good monk. So, this seems to have served as both a temple and a pagoda – a temple in honour of the revered monk. In pagodas, the three Buddhas normally sit in ever-rising ranks in a central position or in a row at the highest rank at the back of the hall of worship.

The small temple off to the left looks like a family chapel, dedicated to the holy mothers, their wooden statues adorned in red, green and white silk gowns, their hair artfully styled under head drapes. Numerous statues of imminent personages crowd the space beneath the holy mothers' glass case, difficult to distinguish as the temple is unlit.

Almost next door to the Ly Quoc Su pagoda, under a large Benjamin fig tree, is a famous open-faced *banh goi* snack shop. *Banh goi* are fried pillows like mini-Cornish pasties, stuffed with pork and spices. And very good they are, too.

Across the street, a few steps further along from Ly Quoc Su pagoda, the Phu Ung temple (between 25 and 25A Ly Quoc Su), was set up by people from Phu Ung village when they migrated here to make wood blocks. It honours Pham Ngu Lao, a native of Phu Ung village, the son-in-law of General Tran Hung Dao, who had been much impressed by the younger man's bravery. High praise indeed from the military hero who saw off the Mongolians in the thirteenth century.

Jolly painted dragons cover the altar of the first temple. At 9.30 a.m. a service of gongs and chanting is in progress. An elderly man leads me past the gaggle of women seated on the floor of the temple to the innermost back temple where a splendid life-sized statue of the moustached General Tran Hung Dao stands in full gilt armour between smaller seated statues of his wife on the left, his sister on the right – the only time I have even seen a wife or a sister depicted in a temple.

It is said that the eighteenth century poet, Ho Xuan Huong, known for her witty, suggestive poetry, had a tea shop somewhere in this same street, but I am unable to find out where. Ho Xuan

Huong's popular poetry, throwing off the restrictions of the Confucian traditions of the time, ridiculed the religious life and anyone in authority. She strongly supported the idea that women should not be subordinate to men and she was resolutely set against multiple wives. Her poetry played on the puns and double meanings of tonal Vietnamese, was always subtle, never vulgar, but very irreverent and sensuous. For the first time, she dared to express a woman's feelings of sensuality. Translation, perforce, tends to be less allusive, more explicit and blatantly direct, of necessity having to choose one meaning when there may be a choice or echoes of several.

The jack fruit is a large roundish fruit with rough, nubbly skin that grows directly from the tree trunk. Its bright yellow pulp has thick, sticky juice.

The Jack Fruit

My body is like the jack fruit, prickly skin, thick pulp,
dear friend, if you like it, drive a wedge into it,
don't touch it, your hands will be slimed all over.

Compassion is a cardinal virtue in Buddhism and the Western Shore is a reference to Buddhist paradise.

The Licentious Monk

A lifetime of abstinence, heavy as a load of stones,
Then only a little slip-up, a mere nothing!
The boat of compassion would have safely reached
the Western Shore,
If some mischievous wind had not come
and tumbled about my rigging.

To Share a Husband

To share a husband with another . . . what a life!
The one sleeps under the covers, well snuggled in,
the other freezes,

By chance he comes across you in the dark,
once or twice a month . . . nothing!
You hang on hoping to get your share,
but the rice is poor and underdone.
You work like a drudge, save that you get no pay,
Ah, had I known it would be like this,
Willingly would I have stayed alone just as I was before.
            (Ho Xuan Huong married twice.)

Night Weaving

Light up the lamp . . . what exquisite fairness!
The stork's bill does not cease to hop all the night
through
Limbs go to work and then relax, all with a lively will,
The shuttle does the weaving, full joyfully applied.
Wide, narrow, small or big, the dimensions always fit;
Short or long, if the part is good, it goes.
For the one who likes a perfect job, let him dip full
good and long
Three falls you need to come and go before the true
colour comes.

In a strictly Confucian moralistic society, Ho Xuan Huong even dared to defend unmarried mothers, twisting a popular proverb into:

To marry and have a child, how banal!
But to be pregnant without the help of a husband,
what an achievement!

(I am indebted to Nguyen Khac Vien and Huu Ngoc for their translations, published in *Vietnamese Literature,* English translation, 1981).

Of all the Vietnamese dead and gone, I think it is Ho Xuan Huong with whom I would most like to share a dinner.

The property along Nha Chung, which translates as Common House, became church property, hence its name. On the right, a bit before the south end of Nha Chung, is a beautifully restored

Neo-Classical French colonial villa with formal gardens, formerly the archbishop's residence, now the Hoan Kiem Library.

The triangular park at the south end of Nha Chung is known as Tay Son Square. By the late eighteenth century, the Nguyen lords as governors in Hue – before they seized power as emperors – had incurred the wrath of the people by levying too heavy taxes. From a family of merchants in the South, three Tay Son brothers mounted a rebellion (1774-1778), first against the Nguyen lords, who they assassinated; then they marched their army north to Thang Long in 1786 to defeat the Trinh lords. Finally, they fought the Qing Chinese, who had opportunistically detected a moment of weakness in the Le dynasty. The three brothers, lead by Nguyen Hue, based their troops outside the Tuyen Vo gate of the Trinh's palace, site of this triangular park.

Nguyen Hue defeated the Chinese in 1788, crowned himself Emperor Quang Trung and married Princess Ngoc Han, a girl of sixteen and the favourite daughter of the weak, former Le emperor, Hien Tong.

As emperor, Quang Trung ruled for only four years before he died at the age of forty in 1792. Some say he was poisoned. Yet despite the age gap and the obvious political advantage of marrying the daughter of the deposed ruler, the marriage must have been a happy one, for the young queen, a widow at twenty, expressed her grief at his death in a now famous poem.

Wind pours its cold into the room
Orchids wither on the veranda
Smoke covers the crypt of the deceased,
The shadow of the royal coach is gone.
Alone, I weep over my fate.
Heaven, why did you shatter our union?
How to tell my misery, my pain
Deep as the ocean, boundless as the sky,
I look to the East, sails glide in all directions,
I see only immensity of sky and water.
I look to the West,
Mountains and trees spread as far as the eye can see.
To the South, wild geese wander,
To the North, mist covers forests with a white shroud.
Though I search, the more this separation weighs upon me,

Will my affliction awaken echoes in that far beyond?
I see the moon through sorrow, its brilliance tarnished,
A fine dust veils its silvered glow.
I am ashamed to look at myself in the mirror,
My love shattered, alone, I wander on the deserted shore.
The flowers I look at return my grief.
Camellias cry tears of dew.
Watching the flitting bird, my heart is torn,
A turtle-dove flies solitary, seeking its companion.
Each landscape wears its own desolation,
Where are the joys of former days?
One moment only and the world collapsed,
So life goes, to whom can I complain,
Love and fidelity, as immense as heaven and earth,
My grief grows as my days endure.
To whom may I confide my torment and pain?
Let sun and moon bear witness!
                              (tr Huu Ngoc)

It is thought by some that if the liberal Emperor Quang Trung had lived to rule, say for twenty years, the country might have remained united with the capital – not in Hue – but in Hanoi, or possibly at his family seat in Qui Nhon, south of Hue. Not surprisingly, a huge statue to honour the hero, Nguyen Hue, has been erected where the final battle against the Chinese supposedly took place.

The battlefield lies in the Dong Da area of Hanoi (corner of Thai Thinh and Tay Son Streets) where a mound of earth is said to cover the fallen Chinese soldiers. Behind a megalithic statue of Nguyen Hue stands a crowded *bas relief* tableau in the style of Social-Realism.

Foot soldiers of the Chinese army march to a drumbeat in strict formation as if passing on parade, their swords held high. Others advance on horseback, beneath flowering peach blossoms, symbol of spring and the Vietnamese New Year *(Tet)*, when the battle took place. So *Tet* offensives were not a new idea in 1968.

Cannons menace the Tay Son peasant soldiers, armed with bows and arrows, signalled by a man blowing a curved buffalo horn. Nguyen Hue commands from the back of an elephant. Following the tableau like a scroll, a little further along to the right lies a scramble of fallen Chinese and a scene of grateful Tay Son soldiers, giving thanks for their victory, backed by a cluster of women, who no doubt supported the army by carrying baskets of infamous *banh chung* cakes (more of which later).

On the fifth day after Vietnamese New Year *(Tet),* a festival is held here to commemorate Nguyen Hue's victory, as well as a somewhat magnanimous ceremony of absolution for the enemy soldiers killed in battle. The hero's palanquin is carried from Khuong Thuong communal house nearby to the temple beside the burial mound. Straw torches and a dragon dance remind observers of the army's use of torches during the battle, their bobbing movements alluding to the undulations of a dragon.

The little triangular park, Tay Son Square, commemorates the hero, Nguyen Hue, Emperor Quang Trung, who unified the country from Qui Nhon northward for the first time and liberated the people from the worst repression of feudalism.

In the old days under French rule, Trang Thi Street at the base of the triangle, ran straight west to the southern gate of Thang Long's citadel. For a time, when the French reasserted their power in Hanoi after World War II, they called this street America Street (Pho My Quoc). Following the French defeat at Dien Bien Phu (1954), it was renamed Trang Thi (Examination Site).

A HIDDEN PAGODA

For the bird, its nest
For man his ancestors
– Vietnamese proverb

Another short detour to a pagoda you would otherwise never find, tucked away behind the shops at the south end of Hoan Kiem Lake, a huge pagoda equivalent to a large parish church for the Hoan Kiem neighbourhood.

It was late one misty night, walking back from a Vietnamese lunar New Year *(Tet)* party, that I was first shown Vu Thach pagoda by a Buddhist friend. One approach is from Ba Trieu Street, alongside a Taoist temple where a sign reads: *Di Tich* (historic relic), *Dinh* (community hall), *Den* (temple), *Chua* (pagoda), *Da Xep Hng Cam Vi Pham* (registered by the government). Happily, the government has recognised the value of the country's religious antiquities. At the end of the alley from Ba Trieu Street, an amateur hand had painted a sign on the wall of the public bathhouse: *su chua, do dien* – with an arrow.

In the lower altar room, we passed a gaggle of old ladies drinking tea, the walls lined with stone memorial tablets, some etched with photographs of the dead of the 'parish', giving it the eerie feeling of a crypt. Others were numbered – reserved for future use.

Climbing the stairs, we slipped out of our shoes into straw slippers and were greeted by an elderly man, who turned on the lights – he turned out to be the head monk out of uniform. To my blinking amazement, this was an enormous pagoda, thick red-lacquered columns, altars and beyond, rising in ranks progressively higher were a dozen or so magnificent, red-lacquered Buddhas, who despite their benign expressions in the dark of night under the glare of electric lights, looked more like devils than saints. Very individual statues, like an un-matching set of giant chessmen, sat along both sides of the pagoda – *arhats?*

'*Arhats* are monks who have not yet reached enlightenment,' my friend explained. 'They appear in pagodas in many different styles, ideally in a band of eighteen, sometimes fewer. They may be elegant and distinguished, amazingly life-like, or pale, plump-faced primitives. They may be seated in a variety of formal Buddhist postures or slouched as if they are lounging under the village banyan tree for a neighbourly chin-wag. Sometimes, several are standing, or the entire set might be riding buffaloes or a variety of beasts – sometimes mythical. They may be covered in gilt, lacquer, brightly painted or of natural wood.

'A pagoda's statues are one of the factors that contribute to its importance. A pagoda may be famous for its antiquity, for its architecture, for its fine sculpture, for the distinguished monks who have presided over it – or who currently preside – or for the personages to whom the adjoining temples are dedicated. Temples as opposed to pagodas, are dedicated to mortals elevated to 'sainthood' for their good work as heroes or heroines, though just occasionally, temples have even been dedicated to scoundrels, thieves or beggars!'

So, like the Catholic church, Buddhism has 'saints'.

Historically, the defeat of the (Confucian) Chinese in the tenth century heralded a golden age of Buddhism in Vietnam from the eleventh to fourteenth centuries, when there was a proliferation of pagoda building. From the fifteenth century, Confucian ideology again dominated, although Buddhism continued concurrently.

The practical-minded Viets were originally animists, worshipping natural forces: the rain god (Phap Vu); the god of clouds (Phap Van); of lightening (Phap Dien) and thunder (Phap Loi), until Buddhism was introduced. Not to waste perfectly good gods, the Viets simply added Buddhist divinities to their indigenous deities. The same happened with Chinese Tao deities such as the emperor of heaven (Ngoc Hoang) and Nam Tao, who registers births, and Bac Dau, who registers deaths.

When I first arrived in Vietnam, as an inveterate temple tramp I had wondered if the old religions would have survived the current political regime. I need not have been concerned. As Vietnamese scholar, Huu Ngoc, so elegantly put it, 'Lying dormant in the subconscious Vietnamese mind is an inclination towards Buddhism, which has been the basis for religion in

Vietnam for eighteen centuries. The Vietnamese are attracted by the preaching of universal compassion rather than karma, non-self and nirvana.'

Uncle Ho has simply been added to the pantheon, and many a plaster bust of the nation's founder adorns a village community hall or temple. That he never married – in a country where everyone marries – merely adds to his mystique, not only as a political, but also as a spiritual leader. (I am assured that he had girlfriends when he was young and certainly, was not homosexual.)

So alongside Communism, which to some is almost a religion, come the first and fifteenth of every lunar month, crowds still troop to pagodas and temples to light joss sticks and make offerings. They climb ridiculously high mountains on pilgrimages and burn votive paper 'pretend' money on the pavement in front of their houses in pursuit of prosperity and happiness. They overlook no holy opportunity to honour Buddha, the Taoist deities, the earlier goddesses, the dead monk patriarchs of the pagodas and any ancient or local personages deified in their temples. And of course, they make offerings to their ancestors at home. So the Vietnamese reluctance to say *no* seems to have applied to religions as they came along. The Vietnamese pragmatically hedge their spiritual bets by appealing to any and all gods. Well, you can't take chances.

Different deities live in different kinds of religious buildings. The communal hall, *dinh* in Vietnamese, is dedicated to the tutelary spirit(s) of the community. The pagoda *(chua)* is reserved for Buddhist worship, although sometimes Taoist statues creep in, especially since bombings, when many pagodas and temples were destroyed and a good many statues have found their way into strictly speaking, inappropriate buildings.

To confuse things further, there are three different kinds of temples: *den* for the cult of heroes or genies; *dien* for the Taoist-tinged worship of spirits and immortals and *van tu* or *van chi* for the cult of Confucius. None of them have convenient signs out front to tell you which they are.

The rectangular hall of a pagoda is divided into two areas: the wide open space for worshippers at the front, the hall of ceremonies *(bai duong)* and the area for altars and statues *(tam boa)* or *(chinh dien)*. Behind the pagoda, usually a separate building, the temple is dedicated to the patriarchs of the pagoda, sometimes to early Buddhas, sometimes Taoist deities.

Many times when visiting pagodas and temples in Vietnam, I have longed for an introduction to the buildings, to the statues and their stories, like the photocopied sheets that English churches sell for a few pence, telling visitors a bit about the church or cathedral. All too often, there is never a monk when you most need one.

At Vu Thach pagoda, the old monk beckoned us to follow him, down a few steps in the dark and around a corner to where he switched on another light. In an alcove was a female *bodhisattva,* holding a baby on her knee. I could make no sense of the old man's toothless French, but later learned that she must have been the Vietnamese Quan Am Thi Kinh, a reincarnation of the Chinese Kwan Yin.

Holding the baby had nothing to do with the birth of Buddha. According to the story, the last trial of a good monk before reaching nirvana is – to endure living one life as a woman. Extending this theory to extremity, there must be a good many, very good women in Vietnam!

But back to the story of Quan Am Thi Kinh. She married, but one night when she attempted to trim one whisker from her husband's chin while he slept, he woke and thinking she was about to slit his throat, beat her and banished her from his home.

The poor wife took refuge in a pagoda disguised as a male monk and was besieged by the unwanted attentions of the village belle, Thi Mau. Despite the monk's rejection, when Thi Mau fell pregnant through another liaison, out of spite she pointed to the monk, who obviously did nothing to support his/her innocence by offering to adopt the baby.

When the monk(ess) finally died, it was discovered that he was a she, and much was made of the wrong that had been done to her. Not surprisingly, having endured this greatest of afflictions and mortifications – life as a woman – the monk(ess) attained nirvana and has since been known as the Vietnamese Quan Am Thi Kinh. That is why she often appears, holding an infant.

In another incarnation, she is the lady of a thousand arms and a thousand eyes, the Vietnamese goddess of mercy. Naturally, she is a very popular goddess, much in demand. Inside the pagoda, a sunburst of gilt surrounded another golden statue of Quan Am

Thien Thu Thien Nhan to give her full name, she of the thousand arms. Two of her hands were in an almost prayerful *mudra* position, slightly open, like a child making a church with a steeple. In one of her many hands, this goddess grasped a spear. Later, a Buddhist friend explained that this statue was probably Tantric, a Tibetan talisman incarnation – 'because a Buddhist Quan Am would never hold a weapon.'

Several tiers of faces made up her crown, representing her thousand eyes to watch over everyone in this world. The slender fingers of her many hands curved in graceful postures and she sat cross-legged in the lotus position, her eyes nearly closed in ecstasy.

We paid tribute to the goddess with a joss stick apiece and returned to the lower level for a chat with an old nun, the monk shutting off the lights behind us. The nun served tea and biscuits and insisted that each of us take a plastic bag containing an orange, an apple and a small packet of biscuits as a kind of benediction. These gifts called *lok* (pronounced luck), my friend explained, would first have been blessed as offerings and remained on the altar at least the length of time it takes to burn a joss stick. I wondered if the street urchins who beg and sell postcards can avail themselves of such *lok*.

The next day, I returned in daylight. Upstairs, just inside the doors of the pagoda, I encounter a giant, glaring temple guardian and four lesser guardians – so much for their guardianship if they had gone unnoticed the night before. Here, instead of writhing with gilt dragons as in a royal palace, the thick red columns are hung with curved boards carved in gilt latticework, inscribed vertically with ideograms – poetic parallel sentences. The old monk is unable to help with the *chu nom* characters.

A curious statue stands beside the first altar. Sometimes I marvel at the obscurity of Vietnamese divinities. This chap, the monk explains, was a very rich man who had many charitable activities, particularly for the poor and orphans, not in this parish, but long, long ago – in India! He was brought to Vietnam as a saint by the Chinese (sic)! The Vietnamese, as they seem to do with travelling deities, welcomed him, took him in, Vietnamised him and added him to their local saints.

In the opposite corner sits pale-faced Duc Thanh Hien, a disciple of Buddha, whose responsibility, apart from keeping his two tiny attendants apart – one righteously white, the other black and evil-looking with grinting green glass eyes – is to deal 'with the 're-education of naughty children.' He also acts as a kind of fortune teller, so during *Tet*, people come to consult him about the New Year. The story goes that he once held a great feast and invited all the wandering souls, poor things, who were so hungry that some of them stuffed themselves fit to burst and a few did – burst! To keep more souls from 'dying' – though I am a little unclear as to how a wandering soul between lives could 'die' – he charged his tiny attendants to drive them out of the feast and perhaps in desolation at his good deed gone wrong, asked that he himself be transformed into a general.

In the daylight I examine the *arhats* along the right wall, not quite a matching set. The first is a tiny gilt statue, seated like a doll in a throne several sizes too big, the baby Sakyamuni, Gaitama Buddha. The second is a bald-pated statue wearing a robe with gracefully carved folds; the third, a thin, elderly *arhat* leaning forward in a posture reminiscent of Rodin's Thinker, but a particularly scrawny and sorrowful Thinker. It was the sculptor, Tran The Koi, who replaces old statues of Buddha in pagodas, who told me about the sad Buddha, who looks down and contemplates the earth's population, as sadly he might. The fourth, fifth, sixth and seventh were identikit *arhats* with pale faces, black lacquer hair and robes. With an ideal total of fourteen, clearly four *arhats* have missed the roll call, or await being donated.

The second altar holds bouquets of flowers and candlesticks.

The first rank of statues look like scholars or graduates, each wearing a tasselled mortarboard, no less personages than the kings of hell – like the *arhats,* there should be ten of them in total – and as might be expected, the hells are ranked, progressively worse and worse. Here there are only two.

When I ask the old monk why such demons are allowed in a pagoda, he explains that in Buddhism, being a compassionate religion, it is the duty of the kings of hell to save the souls of errant sinners – not just to punish them. It sounds like a remarkably benevolent penal code.

The kings stand on either side of an openwork carved gilt grotto, a nine-dragon throne, particular to Vietnamese Buddhism in the North, containing a statue of Buddha as a baby. The function of the nine dragons – always dragons – is to provide ablutions for the newborn babe.

A second tier of Buddhas sit on red-hot lotuses.

At the third level, a huge gilt Buddha daintily holds a lotus blossom in his right hand. A Buddhist friend enlightened me as to its significance. Buddha, during his teaching period, gathered a group of disciples around him. When he plucked the lotus and looked into their faces, one of them smiled knowingly – and Buddha recognized the follower who understood, the follower who would carry on his work.

The statues of the fourth rank wear crowns – *bodhisattvas* – Buddhas who have reached enlightenment, but remained in this world to help others in their religious quest. The one on the right holds a thin-necked vase, to nurture those who have suffered torture; the one on the left, a book, representing knowledge.

Huu Ngoc, humorously acknowledging the simplistic Western mind, describes *arhats* as undergraduates, *bodhisattvas* as having attained a Master's Degree and Buddhas as full-fledged PhDs. The fifth and largest Buddha sits hatless and crown-less, his hair rolled in tight curls with a bump on top. This seated pose of the Buddha in nirvana, the state of enlightenment, is the image that most often appears in Vietnamese pagodas. Above and behind him, three more only slightly smaller, red lacquered Buddhas, sit side by side in the lotus position: Buddhas of the past, present and future. This 'trinity' appears in nearly every pagoda, usually at the top rank.

More attentive *arhats* line the opposite side of the pagoda, first, the fat and happy Buddha, Duc Phat Di Lac, also known as Maitraya. Believers rub his tummy, hoping for prosperity.

The old man had then led us around the corner of the pagoda to an alcove where a statue wearing a crown sat holding a sceptre, the *bodhisattva*, Duc Dia Tang Vuong Bo Tat, who presides over the underworld. It is his duty to save the deceased – but only good Buddhist followers. Note: It takes ten kings of hell to look after the rest. I do a quick body count of statues: inside the pagoda, thirty-three, plus the two tucked in alcoves outside, and this is not even a particularly old nor famous pagoda, little more than a century old.

Up a few steps behind the pagoda is the temple, which my friend explained was 'dedicated to worship of the mother goddesses.' Three golden goddesses sat in regal state in glass cases: goddesses of heaven, forests and waters. Five chaps, sitting in glass cases below, are 'subjects from the court,' accompanied by two cherub-like attendants, minding the brass incense burner and red lacquer candlesticks. A pair of stilt-legged bronze cranes *(ha)* balance on the backs of turtles. The cranes represent the soul, wisdom and longevity and, more practically, operate a flying shuttle-service between earth and heaven for the righteous (live carp carry the kitchen gods).

This is a Tao temple. As I see it, open-mindedness exigency plays an important role in the intermingled religions of Vietnam. Beside the glass cases stand two large painted statues, the first with a puce-pink face, labelled Ban Tran Trieu. The old monk mutters, 'General Tran Hung Dao,' he who defeated the Mongolian hordes – doubtless, after a very long march in the hot sun. On his right sits a pale-faced lady, 'Ban Son Trang,' the Tao goddess of the pure land. Perhaps we should start a Taoist revival to stop pollution. In the opposite corner sits a colossal statue of a bearded monk, 'Bodhidharma, the Indian who founded the Zen sect in China (sic), called Tsien in Vietnam,' joined by two ancestral monks from this pagoda for company.

A double-row of pike-like weapons stand nearby. Originally, my Buddhist friend explained, they represented the symbolic Taoist eight sacred weapons to be applied against the sins of deceit, envy, greed . . . but with the passage of time, they have come to represent the symbols of royal power.

Winding back out of the passageway and crossing the street, I am back beside the lake at Bon Mua cafe for a dish of ice cream, gazing at the picturesque Turtle Tower (Thap Rua), which of course, has a story.

In the Vietnamese scheme of things, the tower is not very old, having been built in 1884 by the mandarin, Ba Kim, who hoped to bury the ashes of his ancestors in this auspicious spot. As it happened, this mandarin, who was in the service of the French district chief, had a daughter who kept a shop on Hong Khay, selling stationery supplies to poor Confucian scholars preparing for their mandarin examinations. The daughter, thinking the students were trying to cheat her, used rude language to the scholars, who retaliated against this daughter of a traitor – serving the French – by ransacking her shop.

52

For a time, the miniature version of the Statue of Liberty was placed on top of Ba Kim's tower – yes, the same Dam Yoe that once stood beside the statue of Paul Bert in Ly Thai To park. In 1886, she had appeared in a collection of 'antiques' displayed at a trade fair to attract investment in Vietnam. Dam Yoe was one lady who got around.

To paraphrase Hanoi historian, Nguyen Vinh Phuc: 'That such a structure as the Turtle Tower, built by a traitor to his country to be put to selfish use, could become a highly emotional symbol evoking the beauty and history of Vietnam's capital city – we forget the origins of the building, mellowed and eroded by time – it has become a part of the soul of Hanoi.'

THE OLD QUARTER OF THIRTY-SIX STREETS

Sell distant relatives to buy near neighbours
– Vietnamese proverb

Think of the oldest civilizations in the world – Greece, India, Egypt, China. Think of old cities such as Athens, Rome, Xian, Cairo. Usually there are no more than a few landmark ruins, an amphitheatre, a temple, a cathedral or a mosque that connects us to past millennia. In few metropolitan conurbations does one feel that the feet of generations have trodden these same streets, century upon century for a thousand years, as one feels in the Old Quarter of Hanoi.

To be sure, the faces of the cities have changed, including Hanoi's, so dramatically that little remains of the deep historic past. Yet Hanoi's Old Quarter, because of its unchanged street patterns, holds tenaciously to its first cultural stirrings in the eleventh century, even though the majority of buildings are no more than a century or two old – with the notable exceptions of tucked-away pagodas, temples, community houses and even a few old shop houses, built and rebuilt in a destructively damp and fluctuating climate. Hanoi's Old Quarter is a compression of concentrated living history at present in a state of rapid flux, a lively study in the evolution of an old cityscape, up to recently, pretty much petrified by the poverty of continuous wars.

As much as I love meandering these highly congested streets, clogged with pedestrians, bicycles, motorbikes, cyclos and the odd taxi, not to mention itinerate vendors, displays of merchandise and shopkeepers squatting with their little dogs on the pavements, it has become so desperately crowded as to feel almost impenetrable. But I dare say, if you appreciate the fussy, busyness of Baroque interiors, Hanoi's life-sized Old Quarter, with its narrow streets and labyrinthine alleys swarming with people and activity, will appeal to your sense of intrigue. It may be present-day, whatever-year, but to worm your way through these lanes is to wander in the footsteps of mandarins and poets, merchants and artisans of the past.

Looking at old photographs of the Old Quarter, I so wish I had lived at least a century ago, to have strolled through this bustling tangle of craft and commercial activity, when people wore black silk 'pyjamas' and straw hats, when rickshaws and palanquins blocked the lanes and the entrances to streets were guarded by thatched gates and night watchmen. Old photographs show that a few of these gates survived well into the French colonial era. As you might suppose, this Old Quarter is the oldest, continuously inhabited urban area in Vietnam. It is certainly the most densely populated in the entire country and reputedly, one of the wealthiest. For most of its thousand years as the capital, the history of Thang Long, later to become Hanoi, was the history of just two areas, the imperial citadel and the civil or commercial quarter, now known as the Old Quarter of Thirty-Six Streets.

When Ly Thai To founded Thang Long in 1010 and built his imperial citadel north-west of Hoan Kiem lake, several religious structures were also built: Dong Co temple (1028) on the To Lich river to the south of West Lake near Pho Thuy Khue, Dien Huu pagoda (One-Pillar Pagoda, 1049), Bao Tien tower (1057, gone) and the Temple of Literature (1070) – three of which (or their derivatives) are still standing. From its founding, Thang Long served as the cultural and intellectual core of the country. Legions of mandarins, monks, scholars and generals who congregated around the court, not forgetting emperors – notably Tran Thanh Ton and Tran Nhan Tong among them – were poets and sometimes historians of note. Chu Van An, a great statesman as well as a poet, served as rector of the Temple of Literature for many years and is still considered to be the father of education in Vietnam. Scholarship was held in very high esteem.

To serve the imperial court, of necessity the commercial quarter was located within easy access of boat transport, the harbours lying along the Red river and the To Lich river, so that goods could be delivered directly to the gates of the royal citadel.

At the beginning, a network of craft villages or representatives of artisan villages, loosely equivalent to guilds, which brought their products to Thang Long's market to sell, grew up between the east wall of the citadel and the Red river. It was first known simply as the market place. In the early days – and still – this area lies in a triangle created by the To Lich river to the west, which formed the eastern moat of the citadel, running from the south-west into the Red river; the Kim Nguu river in the south, which ran east-west along the north shore of Hoan Kiem lake; and the Red river in the east. The To Lich and Kim Nguu rivers have been almost entirely filled in. To the west around West Lake were farms and a fishing industry.

The city of Thang Long, which had a perimeter of thirteen miles (20 km), was protected within earthen walls and Dai La dyke, built sufficiently wide for horse carts and elephants to move along. Outside each gate to the citadel, a large open-air market appeared. In the early days, the bank of the Red river lay further inland, the river having shifted its course to the east as the river silted up. Historically, there were four harbours along the Red river (Song Hong). Ten villages shared the sandy bank of the Red river – outside the gates, the land lying between the city ramparts and the river. As late as the end of the nineteenth century, present-day Nguyen Huu Huan Street, the street of city gates in the Le era (1428-1527), still formed the eastern wall of the city ramparts. The earliest earthen city walls built during the Ly dynasty had twenty brick gates with wooden doors, locked and guarded at night. Visitors had to produce permits and paperwork for the guards in order to be admitted. Taxes were levied and collected on merchandise: fish sauce from Thanh Hoa and Nghe An, salt from seaside regions, bamboo and rattan from the mountains and clay jars from Bat Trang village. All were trundled through the gates of Thang Long.

Later, during the nineteenth century Nguyen dynasty, there were only sixteen gates and still later, only fifteen. Of those fifteen, six or more were on the east side of the commercial side of the city, facing the wharves. A more recent dyke has been built along what is now Tran Nhat Duat, the street name changing to Tran Quang Khai and finally to Tran Phan Du. A marching song sung by the jungle fighters, returning in triumph to Hanoi from their victory at Dien Bien Phu, mentioned the last city gates within living memory: 'They'll enter the city by five gates.'

In the commercial quarter, each of the artisan guild communities of tight-knit villagers was protected by impressive gates or at least bamboo hedges at each end of their 'street', guarded by a watch hut. Today, streets in the Old Quarter still have a habit of changing names every fifty meters or so at the beginning and end of each 'village'. At first, houses were one storey high with thatch or tile roofs – not to exceed the height of the emperor's citadel and windows opening no higher than 'palanquin level' – out of respect to the emperor. No one should peer down at his passing entourage.

Under the first independent Vietnamese dynasties, the Ly and Tran (eleventh to fourteenth centuries), there were sixty-one wards or village streets, each named after the trade or craft practiced there. Most of these street names still start with *pho,* which means street and *hang,* which translates as merchandise or shop. For example, silversmiths from Hai Duong province occupied Pho Hang Bac – *bac* means silver. Below is a list of their names:

Bat Dan	wooden bowls
Bat Su	china bowls
Cha Ca	roasted fish
Chan Cam	string instruments
Cho Gao	rice market
Gia Ngu	fishermen
Hai Tuong	sandals
Hang Bac	silversmiths
Bang Be	rafts
Hang Bo	baskets
Hang Bong	cotton
Hang Buon	sails
Hang But	brushes
Hang Ca	fish
Hang Can	scales
Hang Chai	bottles
Hang Chi	threads
Hang Chieu	mats
Hang Chinh	jars
Hang Cot	bamboo lattices
Hang Da	leather
Hang Dao	(silk) dyers
Hang Dau	beans or oils
Hang Dieu	pipes
Hang Dong	copper
Hang Duong	sugar
Hang Ga	chicken

Hang Gai	silk
Hang Giay	paper or shoes
Hang Hanh	onions
Hang Hom	cases
Hang Huong	incense
Hang Khay	trays
Hang Khoai	sweet potatoes
Hang Luoc	combs
Hang Ma	votive papers
Hang Mam	pickled fish
Hang Manh	bamboo screens
Hang Muoi	salt
Hang Ngang	transversal street
Hang Non	hats
Hang Phen	alum
Hang Quat	fans
Hang Ruoi	clam worms
Hang Than	charcoal
Hang Thiec	tin
Hang Thung	barrels
Hang Tre	bamboo
Hang Trong	drums
Hang Vai	cloth
Lo Ren	blacksmiths
Lo Su	coffins
Ma May	rattan
Ngo Gach	bricks
Thuoc Bac	herbal medicine

By the thirteenth century, the craft guilds had developed sufficiently to satisfy the court's demanding requirements for highly refined, quality products. During the Le dynasty, fifteenth to eighteenth centuries, the commercial area between the Red river wharves and the citadel was reorganized into thirty-six wards, although some suggest that the number thirty-six was merely a symbolic concept as the number nine in Asia symbolizes 'plenty' and nine times four – the four cardinal directions – makes thirty-six, to translate simply as 'many'. There are far more than thirty-six streets in the Old Quarter today and there have been for a very long time.

Each craft village brought along its craft's founder, honoured as a patron saint or deity in the village's communal house, so each street boasted at least one or two religious structures, a pagoda and a communal house, possibly also a temple. The Vietnamese differentiate their religious structures into pagodas *(chua)*, temples *(den)*, village communal houses *(dinh)*, shrines *(mieu)*, chapels for ancestor worship *(nha tho ho)* and congregational houses, though without asking, it is sometimes well nigh impossible for a foreigner to differentiate one from another.

By the fifteenth century, there were still few real streets in Hanoi as we think of streets. Dating back to the thirteenth century, Hang Be, Bang Bac and Hang Dao are probably the oldest. The streets remained small clusters of families, clans, working together at a single craft along dirt lanes, ankle-deep in mud during the monsoon season, dusty in the dry. One begins to appreciate the merit of horse-drawn carts or even palanquins, and later, rickshaws – for the passengers.

International trade arrived as early as the thirteenth century with traders from China – who were already there – and Java as well as monks from India. The seventeenth century brought a broadening of international trade through Portuguese, Dutch and French traders, along with refugees from China, fleeing the defeat of the Ming. The craft streets, which originally had been no more than temporary thatched market stalls, had slowly evolved into long narrow 'tube' houses, sometimes no more than two or three metres wide, going back sixty meters or more, broken up by open courtyards for light and ventilation. Shops were taxed by the width of frontage to the market; living space was pushed to the back and eventually to upper floors. Courtyards in between the front shop and back residential houses were used for washing and drying, preparing food, sometimes cottage industries, as well as places to enjoy hobbies, a bird collection, a tiny garden of potted decorative plants, a rock garden or a fish pond.

As time went on, wealthy merchants began to build more permanent shops and warehouses of brick with sloping two-tiered, tile roofs, the tiles coming from Bat Trang village. Some of these beautiful old tile roofs remain, covered in moss, in the oldest streets such as Hang Buon, Hang Bac, Hang Be and Ma May. The fronts of the houses had removable wooden slats so that the front rooms could be closed or opened to be used as shops. Hang Ngang Street, where the Chinese community from Canton settled, was even paved with marble.

Despite the shift of political power in 1802 when the Nguyen dynasty assumed power and moved the capital down country to Hue, Thang Long remained a commercial centre. The eastern wall of the new fortress-citadel built by the Nguyens was a bit further west from the original citadel's east wall, freeing space for new streets. It was in 1831 that the Nguyens changed the name of Thang Long to Hanoi.

North of Hoan Kiem Lake in the Old Quarter, which the French called the native quarter, the thicket of narrow streets and alleys continued to grow, seemingly haphazardly. Most of the buildings in the Old Quarter of today as well as many streets around the cathedral, date from the late nineteenth and early twentieth century up to the 1930s – those that haven't been rebuilt completely in the past ten years. In more or less French style, many are of brick and cement, two storeys high with tall louvered windows, shutters and curved balconies with balustrades. But the old street patterns, the narrow alleys and inner, hidden-away courtyards remain. During the war against the French, many of these old streets were barricaded and the walls pierced to give the Viet Minh access to escape from one building or street to another. Numerous murderously close-range battles were fought in the Old Quarter of Thirty-Six Streets.

From an architectural point of view, the poverty of Vietnam after World War II (1945), after Dien Bien Phu (1954), during the Vietnam War (1965-1975) and up to the introduction of the *doi moi* renovation policy of 1986, which slowly opened Vietnam to commercial activity, personal enterprise and foreign investment as opposed to collective farming, state-run factories and trade, meant stagnation in building, not only in Hanoi but throughout Vietnam. As a result, many of these old buildings have survived, their unpainted louvered shutters sagging, their ochre walls stained by the rains of many monsoons. Only in the last ten years have the Vietnamese begun to have enough money to rebuild their shop house homes, sometimes shooting up four or five storeys to accommodate mini-hotels. Many of the original trades have gone, but the tradition of specialist trades in certain streets lives on and the social cohesiveness of generations of people from the same village living cheek-by-jowl in one small area, a legacy of the village guild system, remains.

It is thought that professional craft workers now only make up less than eight per cent of the population of the Old Quarter. Traders make up half.

According to statistics, the Old Quarter is home to 15,270 households, 60 percent having resided there for more than thirty years, many for generations.

In 1999, Hanoi's People's Committee drew up Temporary Regulations on Management of Construction, Preservation and Restoration of Hanoi's Old Quarter. The document specified the Old Quarter as an area of one hundred hectares (247 acres) and according to the official count – having seventy-six streets – with the borders running along: Phung Hung Street in the west; Hang Bong, which changes to Hang Gai, Cau Go and Hang Thung Streets in the south; Tran Quang Khai, changing to Tran Nhat Duat Streets in the east.

The regulations specify which houses and buildings of historical and cultural interest are to be preserved and include rules for upgrading, building materials and colours. Sloping roofs of traditional Vietnamese tiles are allowed, but no reinforced concrete. Regulations allow for the modernization of interiors, but specify strict control over facades and limit the extension of balconies and roofs. Furthermore, the city plans to improve drainage and replace the snarl of electric and telephone wires overhead with underground cables. And a new lighting system with sodium or high-tension-filament lamp-posts will replace fluorescent lighting. So far, the snarls of overhead wires remain.

The traffic? Certain streets have been designated one-way, numerous traffic lights have been installed and a few junctions even have traffic wardens with little red flags to help pedestrians cross the street.

The authorities are doing what they can to preserve the architectural fabric of the Thirty-Six Streets. Seventy-nine historic, cultural and religious sites, including sixty temples have been designated, along with 859 'valuable architectural sites': 245 'ancient' and 614 'old houses'. After all, the Old Quarter of Thirty-Six Streets is not only the oldest part of Hanoi, it is the oldest surviving neighbourhood in the country and Hanoi's most precious historic heritage.

A STROLL THROUGH THE OLD QUARTER

When the lamp goes out,
the hut and the brick house look alike
– Vietnamese proverb

Hanoi's Old Quarter of Thirty-Six Streets is the liveliest urban maze I know, a constantly vibrant microcosm of Vietnamese city life. As you pick your way carefully around parked motorbikes, people squatting on tiny plastic stools at pavement cafes – locals call them 'dust cafes' – wandering vendors balancing carrying poles and merchandise being unloaded, don't forget to look up. Soaring above the old two-storey shop houses, it's a wonder that these new five and six-storey buildings, sometimes no more than three meters (9 feet) wide, don't need flying buttresses.

Countless cyclo and *xe om* (motorbike taxis) will offer their services – the polite negative response is thank you, *com un.* Arriving is unimportant, wandering slowly and looking is. Resign yourself to getting happily lost. The bends, diagonals and dead ends of these lanes seem intentionally to ignore the cardinal compass points. Yet streets are well marked; most shops display their addresses. In extremity, just mutter 'Hoan Kiem' and someone will cheerfully point you towards the lake.

In earlier times before the French, just north of Hoan Kiem were two more lakes, Hang Dao and Thai Cuc. Bountiful with fish, Thai Cuc was connected to Hoan Kiem by a small stream over which there was a wooden bridge. Vendors along the bank sold fish caught in the lake – the fish market.

It is so easy in these busy, congested streets to miss a small community house or a pagoda. To understand a bit of what you are seeing while strolling these old streets, it is useful to have an inkling of their history – the stories, the derivation of their names, the products that were originally produced in each one, and how they have evolved from their original functions. Delving into their origins is therefore an absorbing adventure into the past. So for the stroller or the armchair traveller –

Walk north, along HANG DAO

Hang Dao Street is one of the busiest streets in the Old Town – and that is saying something – its shops bursting with Western style clothes, shopkeepers busily loading and unloading their produce, motorbike shoppers paused in the street. It is also one of Vietnam's oldest streets and one of the main north-south axes dividing the Old Quarter. Originally, Hang Dao Street formed part of the dyke bordering Thai Cuc Lake. Even as recently as the dawn of the nineteenth century, perhaps only a hundred houses lined Hang Dao, most still of woven straw and palm leaves, only a few of brick.

Dao means pink, the colour of peach blossoms, the symbol of spring and the lunar New Year *(Tet)*. The Hang Dao guild of silk dyers produced a special pink dye and at first, Hang Dao was the place where silk was brought for dyeing. Other shops for dark brown dyeing were in Dyers Street, Tho Nhuom.

Each shop had a carved wooden or tin animal sign hanging out front to identify the shop or its specialty for those illiterate in Chinese ideograms. The front room of shops held display cases and a smiling woman inside to attract customers. In the innermost compartment, the owner sat on a wooden bed, surrounded by bolts of brocade, flowering satins and fine silk gauze.

By the turn of the twentieth century, Hang Dao and Hang Bac were the most prosperous streets in Hanoi. Wealthy silk and gold merchants married their daughters to poor, well-connected scholars, studying to become mandarins in order to gain access to the intellectual aristocracy – social climbing. This tradition continued well into the 1940s, the theory being that busy wives as shopkeepers or money changers were ideal for idle, lazy husbands. There was even a saying: 'Who marries a scholar, marries a man with a long back, who doesn't do anything useful' – his long back from bending over his books and calligraphy.

Shops sold all manner of silk, brought to Thang Long from the villages where it was woven: semi-transparent silk called *the* from La village; *linh* satin from Buoi, south of West Lake; rough *choi* from Phung; transparent *van,* flowering silk and crepes from Van Phuc in Ha Dong; *nhieu* brocade from around Mo village; raw silk and silk floss *dui* from Dai Mo; raw silk *gan* and silk floss *dui* from Dai. Silk weaving was and remains, astonishing specialized.

Crowded silk fairs took place the first, sixth, eleventh, twenty-first and twenty-sixth of each lunar month when representatives from the weaving villages came to Thang Long to give orders to the dyeing villages. Apart from a few silk jackets and *ao dais* in deep hued colours, hanging among the Western style clothes, most of the silk trade has now shifted to Pho Hang Gai (more of which later).

Following World War I, merchants from France, India and Pakistan arrived in the Thirty-Six Streets, bringing imported fabrics. It was this group of Muslim traders who established their mosque on Pho Hang Luoc.

A fine historic building at 38 Hang Dao, offices of the Hanoi Ancient Quarter Management Department, has been restored and is now open to the public. In 1941, the private owners rebuilt the house and added a story. The ground floor had been originally used as living quarters for the family, who kept their family altar on the first floor. The house retains a seventeenth century stone stele with Chinese ideograms from a communal house and a carved altar featuring a dragon, a phoenix, a crane and a turtle.

CAU GO
Off to the right, Cao Go Street marks the former site of the little wooden bridge over the Kim Nguu river. The near (west) end of the street used to be the area for bleaching and dying silk; the east end sold dry palm nuts *(cau)* from the areca palm, one of the ingredients for chewing betel. The French filled in Thai Cuc lake and the stream connecting it to Hoan Kiem. You may notice that the foundations of some of the houses on the north side of Cao Go Street are lower than the road – they were built in the former lake bed and over the years, have settled.

Not quite a century ago, Cau Go had a reputation for good noodle soup *(pho,* pronounced foo as in foot) shops. Number 106 in a nineteenth century building (now offices) was the site of one of the first *pho* shops in the vicinity.

At one time, the street housed workshops building carriages, both horse-drawn and man-drawn. Six or seven families cooperated in producing the various parts: canopies, leather seats, wheels, frames. Number 37 Cau Go (now a print shop) is a historic site. From 1930 to 1945, it was the hideout of the anti-French, Love the Country Movement. During the French Indo-

Chinese War, the Viet Minh held this street until February 1947, when they withdrew to the countryside to fight a guerrilla war. Oh yes, the Vietnamese and their ancestors, the Viets, have practiced guerrilla warfare for more than two thousand years.

The entrance to Cau Go Alley (Wooden Bridge Alley) is a colourful flower market. Walking north along Hang Be, two streets further (north) we come to . . .

HANG BAC
One of the oldest, if not *the* oldest of Thang Long's old streets, dating from the thirteenth century. For centuries, Hang Bac has been the centre for jewellery, the gold and silver trade and money exchange. Now, it is crowded with tourist cafes and craft shops; the jewellery shops start on the extension of the street, west of Dinh Liet.

The Viet tribes living in the area of Hanoi first used metallurgical techniques as early as three thousand years ago during the Dong Son Bronze Age. Centuries later, in the reign of Le Thanh Tong (1460-1497), the minister of the Interior, Luu Xuan Tin, received imperial permission to bring metal workers from his village, Trau Khe. He set up a silver ingot factory at 58 Hang Bac (now a travel agent). At first they cast ingots, later coins. The Upper Tren communal house at numbers 50-58 served as a school for training apprentice silversmiths. The Lower Kim Ngon communal house at numbers 42-48, (still a community meeting room with a bust of Ho Chi Minh), was the foundry where molten silver was poured into moulds.

Later, when merchants needed large amounts of money and metal coins or bars were too heavy, an exchange on Hang Bac would be arranged. The gold and silver dealers of Hang Bac were therefore, the forerunners of bankers. Even today, the word for paper money is *bac,* meaning paper silver and occasionally, the jewellers of Hang Bac still change money (dollars in preferably large denomination bills). In the eighteenth century, the street attracted jewellery designers from Dinh Cong village, south of Hanoi. Three brothers, the patron spirits of jewellery makers in Vietnam, learned their trade in China in the sixth century. A temple dedicated to them is locked away at 84 Hang Bo Street, the western extension of Hang Bac (a friendly lady tells me to come back later).

Much wholesale trade in gold, silver and semi-precious gems still takes place in Hang Bac and Hang Bo and the busy wholesalers can seem a bit brusque. Their showcases are full of gold and jade rings, bangle bracelets and the occasional glass counter displays the thick, solid gold necklaces that still form the dowry of the wealthy Hanoi bride.

Hang Bac had its share of stories and eccentrics. Miss Be Ti, who lived in Hang Bac, was always euphemistically called 'the little girl from Hang Bac,' although in reality she was a rather fat lady. She ran a money brokerage, but people came from afar to see her zoo: a four-legged chicken, a pig with two mouths and a couple of deformed dwarfs. Hang Bac was also the setting for a short story, *Meo Lua,* from *Essays in the Rain* by Pham Dinh (1768-1839). In the story –

The palanquin of a great mandarin's wife made a noisy entry into Dong Lac guild. The palanquin, preceded and followed by a swarm of lackeys and guards, had blinds made of painted jackdaw's wings. The entourage stopped in front of the goldsmith's shop, the servants were ordered to negotiate to buy several dozen silver *taels* (a former measure of weight for precious metals). Hardly was the haggling finished when the lady, who remained in her palanquin, told an old servant to take ten *taels* to the palace so that her husband could give his advice on the price. The goldsmith suspected nothing amiss in this. An instant later, without warning, the entire retinue, including the two carrier guards disappeared. At sundown, as the old servant had not brought back the ten *taels* of silver, the goldsmith went to the palanquin to reclaim his property. Upon opening the blinds, enthroned inside he found only a dazed, old blind beggar woman in a red crepe tunic. Investigations into the matter were inconclusive. The dilapidated palanquin was worth no more than a few coins.

The Golden Bell Theatre at the corner of Hang Bac and Dinh Liet (where it joins Ta Hien), was built in 1920 by a Chinese merchant for performances of *cai luong* musical theatre. *Cai luong* (see later chapter) employs elements of both Vietnamese traditional opera *(tuong)* and folk opera *(cheo)*. A relatively modern theatrical form first created in the South in the nineteenth century, *cai luong's* farcical over-drawn characters make the plots very easy to follow without knowing a word of Vietnamese and the music, even to the Western ear, can be quite entrancing. (No one at the theatre speaks English, but the shop girl opposite will inquire for you about performances).

It was on the steps of this theatre on 14 January 1937, during the war against the French that the Hanoi guards, a unit of the anti-French resistance force, swore 'to fight to the death.' Their headquarters at 86 Hang Bac (now a craft shop), was then the home of Chan Hung, the largest goldsmith shop on the street. Sadly, beneath the ornate crest and once elegant balconies, it is now difficult to tell which is the peeling paint of the facade, the ochre or the rust-red.

In its Hanoi 2010 Project, Hanoi Ancient Quarter Management Department is busy restoring old buildings. Number 47 Hang Bac and numbers 97 and 99 (at the corner of Ha Tien, opposite the Cai Luong Theatre), are scheduled for renovation.

A little further east at the corner of Hang Bac and Hang Be, stone masons tap away, chipping the photographs of the dearly departed onto memorial stones. Back-tracking, turn right into . . .

MA MAY

The temple at number 64 (corner of Luong Ngoc Quyen), dating from 1450, is dedicated to Nguyen Trung Ngan (1289-1370), an early governor of Thang Long and according to the stele: 'This temple was built in the Tran Dynasty.' It is locked, but one can peer through the open, wooden grill gate to see the red and gold gilt altar.

At one time this street was divided into two streets: Hang May (south) selling rattan and Hang Ma (north) selling religious paper votive objects for burning: paper money, paper suits of clothes, hats, even life-sized rattan and straw animals, used for religious offerings.

At the end of the nineteenth century, the French set up a customs office – then just outside the East Gate (Quan Chuong) – a court house and a prison at numbers 19 and 33, respectively. Now a lacquer shop and a travel agent, the two ochre-painted buildings are just recognizable.

Under the French, the Vietnamese called Hang Ma, Black Flag Street, as the Black Flags, a secret Chinese society, had its headquarters here. The Black Flags, a roving anti-colonial military unit from South China led by Luu Vinh Phuc, who had fled to Vietnam when the Manchus took over Hunnan, joined the Vietnamese in resisting when the French were first trying to gain control of Vietnam in the 1880s. It was they who attacked the small French church, Chapelle des Martyrs, in Nha Chung Street when the priests took refuge in Ba Da pagoda, around the corner. The French called them *pavillons noir,* black pirates.

The Hanoi Ancient Quarter Management Department has already completed renovation of the old building at 47 Hang Ma – and re-installed a granny.

Number 87 Ma May, the former residence of a Chinese merchant, has been beautifully restored by the city of Toulouse and is now open as a museum. Past the dark wooden stools and tea table, past the calligraphy, lacquer boxes and ceramics for sale, through an open courtyard with a hammock and caged birds, is the former kitchen. Upstairs at the front of the house is the beautifully carved family altar, a carp scroll on the left, a peacock on the right. The pretty young guide says the altar is only a century old. (The lacquer statues along the wall are all for sale).

An open courtyard separates the altar room from 'the women's workroom.' I note the carved eaves beneath the tile roofs and the carved wooden doors that can be closed in winter. The bedroom beyond holds beautiful inlaid mother-of-pearl cabinets. This would have been the home of a wealthy merchant during a time when even the wealthy lived in what we would consider quite spartan conditions.

At the far end of the street, Hang Ma curves into . . .

HANG BUON

By the mid-eighteenth century, Hang Buom had become almost a self-contained community of Chinese from Canton selling mostly agricultural products, rice and sugar as well as fruits imported from China. Among those imports was opium on behalf of the French opium monopoly. Following the Treaty of Ports, the British had foisted Indian opium onto the Chinese market. Opium had been prohibited in China for many centuries, and although there was a thriving black market, the Manchu authorities protested at the British import of Indian opium, first in 1840 by dumping chests of imported Indian opium into the harbour, igniting the Opium Wars, then by exporting some of the unwanted evil on to Hanoi.

Hang Buom became an infamous good-time street of opium dens, bars, restaurants, theatres and later, cinemas. Little Sam Cong Alley, off Hang Buom (to the left), was a notorious red light district of brothels. Two carved wooden peaches indicating brothels, hung over many doors. The saying was: 'Hang Buom is a place of drunkenness – drunk in the morning, drunk in the afternoon, drunk in the evening, drunk all the time.' Faintly reminiscent of its colourful past, one building facing Le Maquis Bar still calls itself The Cheeky Quarter. Nestled among the beauty and nail salons, tattoo and massage parlours, the Red Mask and Ha Noi Dramatic Theatre look as though they closed long ago. With the passage of time, the character of the street has changed – the families sitting in front of their shops look remarkably wholesome.

Rather unexpectedly given its proximity, Hang Buom is also the location of one of Hanoi's oldest, most hallowed temples (corner of Hang Boum and Hang Giay). Bach Ma (temple of the White Horse), is Hanoi's guardian temple of the east. Its carved funeral palanquin serves to carry the spirit of the white horse. Confusingly, the temple is also dedicated to the earth spirit, Long Do (the Dragon's Navel), who was the spirit of Mount Nung, the mountain located within the citadel where Long Do (the dragon) allegedly lived. According to legend, the first Ly emperor, Ly Thai To, prayed at this temple in those days dedicated to Long Do, for divine assistance in building the city's ramparts. The walls kept crumbling – not so surprising when attempting to build earthen walls in the alluvial flood plain of a great river in a monsoon climate. His prayers were answered when a white horse appeared and showed him where to place the walls.

The white horse was the messenger of the spirit of To Lich river. Where the white horse paused, temples were built to guard the city: Bach Ma in the east, Kim Lien in the south, Voi Phuc in the west and Quan Thanh in the north. Bach Ma has been rebuilt several times and is in the process of being smartened up as I step through the red lacquered doors of the gate to the sound of sanding and traditional Vietnamese music.

In the courtyard, men are rubbing down, then reapplying red lacquer and gold paint to the parallel sentence panels attached to the pillars of the temple. To the left hangs a huge ceremonial drum, to the right a television set, presumably for the guardian.

A Vietnamese-style rock garden in a pond dominates the right side of the courtyard, backed by a wall where a carp is being transformed into a fiery dragon, floating through clouds, alluding to the Confucian notion that through hard work an ordinary person can become – extraordinary – and rise in the world. Not only were dragons the dual symbol of power and the emperor, but according to the Viet creation myth, the Vietnamese believe that they are the descendants of a fairy and a sea dragon. The creation myth goes like this –

The sea dragon and a fairy married and the fairy laid one hundred eggs. Being celestial, when the eggs hatched, all of the offspring were fully grown. However, the fairy had come from the mountains and the sea dragon, of course, from the sea. When she started to yearn for the mountains and he for the sea, they decided to part, each taking half of their children, with the understanding that if either should ever need help, the other would assist. So, an amicable divorce between mythical beasts. The Viets, now the Vietnamese, believe that they are the descendants of these two mythical parents.

In an update to worship, pyramids of soft drinks stand on the altar dedicated to the jolly, life-sized white horse, kept company by two giant gilt lacquered cranes *(ha)*. The three Taoist holy mothers of sky, water and earth watch from their glass case on the right. To the left, a shrine is dedicated to a Chinese queen of the thirteenth century (Nam Hai Tu Vi Thanh Nuong), who with her child and nanny, threw themselves into the sea to avoid capture by the Mongolians. Since then, she has protected sailors.

In the temple behind, huge china vases and two delightfully comical figures with pot bellies face one another. Later over a coffee, the owner of the nearby Ladybird cafe explains that the old man with the big nose and the jutting chin is the people's hero – deity – for longevity and the other, who holds money in his hand, represents prosperity. Another source suggests that because of their dark skins, they were captured Chams. The Hindu-Buddhist-Islamic kingdoms of Champa to the south and Dai Viet were frequently in conflict during the Ly and Tran dynasties.

In the early days, a live buffalo was sacrificed in Bac Ma temple to ensure a prosperous new year. More recently, a ceremony called Beating the Buffalo took place to signify the end of winter and the beginning of spring. A terracotta buffalo was thrashed with a mulberry branch, then carried ceremonially to the imperial palace. Ironically, when the invading Ming Chinese occupied this street (1407-1427), they used Bach Ma temple to honour Ma Yuan, the very Chinese general who had defeated the heroic Trung sisters, who wrested Vietnamese independence from the Chinese for a brief period (40-43 AD). According to legend, rather than be taken prisoner by the Chinese, the heroic Trung Sisters threw themselves into the Hat Giang river. The Hai Ba Trung temple, dedicated to the brave Trung sisters (located in the south of Hanoi on Pho Tho Lao Street), was founded in 1142.

Strolling west along Hang Buom, I pass the remains of a very old building between numbers 26 and 30 – a project for the Hanoi Ancient Quarter Management Department, perhaps – before turning right into Hang Giay (there are two Hang Giays, one here and one further north); the next street north is . . .

NGUYEN SIEU

The scholar, Nguyen Sieu (1799-1872) for whom the street is named, was a true polymath who wrote books on history, geography, economics, literature and poetry. He lived at numbers 12 and 14 where he opened a school. In the communal house at number 20, there is still an altar to him, although it is now a private house. The street is built on the now covered over To Lich riverbed, virtually at the mouth of the To Lich river where it joined the Red river.

HANG CHIEU

The old East Gate (Quan Chuong), stands at the east end of the next east-west street, Hang Chieu (Rush or Sedge Floor Mats). The unimpressive height of this three-entrance gate makes one wonder who it might have deterred. Yet this was Thang Long's most important city gate, strategically located to control the rice market on the To Lich river. The gate was last renovated in 1817.

In 1749, the city walls had twenty-one gates, including Quan Chuong. By 1831, it was down to sixteen. Each gate had a mandarin in charge of security and collecting taxes.

Quan Chuong, the only gate remaining, was also known as Dong Ha (East River Mouth) – of the To Lich river, and the Military Mandarin gate. In the old days, Quan Chuong gate stood virtually on the bank of the Red river, facing Ben Nua wharf.

71

It holds a stele forbidding the mandarin guards from harassing the free flow of merchandise and funeral processions.

Retracing my steps I turn right into what has become Nguyen Thien (it becomes Hang Giay further south).

DONG XUAN MARKET

In the early days there were two markets nearby, Bach Ma in Hang Buom Street and Cau Dong in Hang Duong Street. However, in 1889, the French filled in the To Lich river and 'cleaned up' the old markets, concentrating them in a fenced-in muddy area of reclaimed land in a former lake bed.

The following year, they built a huge covered market with five entrances. A century later in 1994, a fire destroyed it; it was rebuilt with the original facade as it appears today.

Past the caged birds and carefully stacked fruit at the entrance, including a strange yellow fruit called Buddha's fingers – it looks like a lemon in which the rind grows in segments – past the odoriferous butchers stalls, inside are narrow, tightly packed aisles of dried fruit and sweets, dried mushrooms, beans and seeds, noodles galore, dried fish and shrimp heaped on woven straw platters.

Upstairs is such a tightly packed, jumble of bolts of fabric piled high that I am happy not to be shopping.

These days Don Xuan is more of a wholesale than a retail market, but stall holders will oblige if you need something, sometimes even lead you to where it is.

Back downstairs, through the courtyard which holds bundles of tights, on into the second section of the market, filled with more shoes than I have ever seen in one place, plus bags, socks, towels, stationery, toys, toiletries and knitted hats. I am relieved to escape out the west entrance of the market into Hang Luoc.

From across the street, turning round you can see the facade of the market as the French built it. If you are walking and the market has finished you off, catch a cyclo, agreeing the price before you get in, as there seem to be no convenient restaurants in this highly commercial neighbourhood for a reviving coffee. Otherwise, turn right into Hang Xuan, which walking north becomes Hang Giay – the other Hang Giay . . .

72

SOUTHWEST OF DONG XUAN MARKET

HANG GIAY

During the French era, this Hang Giay was noted for its *H'at A Dao,* female entertainers somewhat similar to Japanese geishas, who performed as solo singers in public houses. The singer's paying patron would beat a tiny drum to register his response. *H'at A Dao* singing of epic poems was named after a famous eleventh century singer. *'H'at'* means singing, *'A'* means Miss and *'Dao',* was the original singer's name. So rather touchingly, *H'at A Dao* means, 'Miss Dao's singing.' The words of a Hanoi folk song run:

> *When we passed Hang Giag,*
> *we could hear the dan day* and the castanets,*
> *So it is spring there in all four seasons.*
> (*Dan day is a stringed instrument).

Reversing my steps along Hang Giay, which becomes Dong Xuan, I turn right into . . .

HANG MA

One of Hanoi's most colourful streets, Hang Ma is still the street to buy votive papers as well as all kinds of paper. The shops are festooned with red silk and paper lanterns, huge red heart-shaped boxes, balloons, glittering tinsel, toys, big red bows, paper garlands, artificial flowers, gift wrappings, ribbons and paper, gilt lilies, artificial fruit and fake money for burning – US dollars, of course. I turn right past the shops selling soft toys into . . .

HANG LUOC

Once a year, a few days before the Lunar New Year *(Tet),* Hang Luoc transforms itself into a flower market selling traditional peach blossoms and kumquat trees, the rather elegant Vietnamese equivalent of Christmas trees for *Tet,* New Year celebrations.

Early in the 1900s, Indian and Pakistani textile traders built a mosque in this street, which locals called the 'pagoda of the black Westerners.' Many Muslims fled south after the French left in 1954 and for a time, it stood unused and vacant. The young students of the Hang Cot School for Girls next door were terrified of the ghosts, haunting it. Now it serves members of the international Muslim business community and Muslim diplomats. Several streets in this area lie in the former To Lich riverbed: Hang Luoc (Combs), Hang Ruoi (Sand Worms), Hang Chai (Bottles), Hang Cot (Bamboo Mats), and Le Van Linh. Up to the nineteenth century, a small canal ran through here, close to the wall of the mosque, a remnant of the To Lich river. Several temples along this stream were dedicated to sea goddesses.

According to legend, during the Tran dynasty, people in Nghe An province fished the bodies of four girls out of the sea. Having buried them, they set up a temple to honour them as the four holy ladies (Tu Vi), praying to them for calm seas. Boats and ships from Nghe An always carried altars dedicated to these four goddesses, so they became widely known. Many temples up and down the coast and more than ten temples along the banks of the To Lich and the nearby Red river honoured these four goddesses, thought to protect sailors at sea.

Number 59 Hang Luoc looks like a pagoda. The door is open, the courtyard is parked full of motorbikes and on one side, a woman is cooking. She motions me to go inside where indeed, there is a statue of Buddha and two crowned figures difficult to discern in the gloom. I slink out as obviously, people are now living here. Hang Luoc imperceptibly turns into Cha Ca . . .

CHA CA
Part of one of the north-south axes running parallel to Hang Dao, fish from the To Lich river used to be sold in Cha Ca. In recent years, the street has become famous for a restaurant serving grilled fish, opened by the Doan family at number 14 and now, there are several competing restaurants along the street, all specializing in grilled fish. A ramshackle building at the corner of Cha Ca and Hang Ca looks like an old temple, but it has obviously become someone's home.

Not to miss a rather special temple in the next street, I turn left along Lan Ong, then left into . . .

HANG DUONG (SUGAR)
In the early days, shops here sold dried, sweetened fruits or vegetables called *mut*. Another specialty of the street was *o mai*, sweetened or salted whole fruit. A few shops in Hang Duong still

sell these delicacies. At 36 Hang Duong, gaily-painted warriors guard the gate of the Cau Dong temple. Inside, women chant to the rhythm of a gong, kneeling on mats at the altar in honour of Ngo Van Long, a general in the reign of Hung Due Vuong – the eighteenth (prehistoric) Hung king!

This is a richly carved gilt temple, as is the adjoining Buddhist pagoda, thick gilt columns and intricate gilt carvings over the altars and doors. Ranks of carved *arhat* statues stand along the side walls beside the altar. An open-work, nine-dragon throne to Buddha as a baby occupies the central altar space, behind which sits a huge placid Buddha having reached nirvana, the topmost rank of statues representing the Buddhas of past, present and future.

A stele of 1624 tells of the rebuilding and expansion by a married monk patron named Nguyen Van Hiep and describes the temple as being located on a beautiful site, 'the Nhi Ha river flowing in front and the Long Bien (imperial) Citadel and mountains behind.' A stele of 1711 announces that Cau Dong was declared a 'specially privileged pagoda.' So it has been considered distinguished for at least three hundred years.

The temple on the left holds four statues, the largest said to represent Tran Thu Do (1194-1254), next to his wife – suggsting that this pagoda and temple are much older than three hundred years old. Tran Thu Do was a powerful political figure, who forced the young daughter of the last Ly emperor to marry his young nephew, Tran Canh, thereby enabling his nephew to seize the throne and establish the Tran Dynasty in 1255.

It has also been written that he was responsible for the previous emperor's assassination in Chan Giao pagoda and for the execution of more than three hundred nobles of the previous regime – the accepted method of ridding yourself of a troublesome previous dynasty. Walking south along Hang Duong, it becomes . . .

HANG NGANG
As early as the Le dynasty when Thang Long was still a new capital, Chinese merchants were allowed to live and trade here. Many, mostly from Canton, lived in Hang Ngang. The oldest houses built in the original style are at numbers 29, 33 and 43 and on the even side, numbers 4 and 52, now a wee, tile-roofed

clothes shop. Although a modern building, number 48 is historically significant. It was here in 1945 that Ho Chi Minh lived and worked in a small room on the third floor, and where he penned the Vietnamese Declaration of Independence, borrowing heavily from the American model. The date celebrated as Vietnam's August Revolution, 19 August 1945, was in fact the date of the Japanese surrender – which signalled the Viet Minh to rush into the temporary power vacuum and seize control of the rural villages of the North. It was also on the second floor of this building that the decision was taken for Ho Chi Minh's Provisional Government to appear in public. Two weeks later on 2 September 1945, Ho Chi Minh read out his new Declaration of Independence in Ba Dinh Square, on the date that subsequently become Vietnam's National Day. There is a plaque in Vietnamese, but the building is closed.

Retracing my steps north on Hang Duong, I turn left into . . .

HANG MA
Walking west to the junction where Hang Dong (Copper) meets Hang Ruoi (Sand Worms) – edible sand worms were sold here in the ninth lunar month, and no, I haven't tried them. They can still be found with determination, I am told, for a brief time in the autumn at Hanoi markets.

On the pavement, a couple of boys are sprinkling silver glitter on cut-out foam stars. Opposite, a funeral marquis, white lilies framing the entrance, covers the pavement in front of one house.

HANG COT
A little further along Hang Ma, Hang Cot (on the right) meets Hang Ga (on the left). Tam Phu temple at 52 Hang Cot is dedicated to the holy mother goddesses of the sky, forests and water. Dragons adorn the tips of the gate roof, carp 'kneel' atop pillars. Painted plaster and silk serpents wrap themselves around the beams supporting the intricately carved arch above the inner entrance to the altar area. Pillars carry heavily encrusted gilt panels; three succeeding altars rise steeply to the figures of the goddesses. As late as the end of the nineteenth century, families living in Hang Cot made bamboo mats *(cots),* used as temporary walls for houses. The streets here, just outside the north-east corner of the citadel, once held many inns of *H'at A Dao* singers.

In the Hang Choi communal house in Hang Cot Alley, which was dedicated to the patron founder of *H'at A Dao* singing, a contest was held annually to which singers came from afar to compete.

HANG GA

Retracing my steps south, Hang Cot becomes Hang Ga. If I were to turn right and walk along Cua Dong for three streets, I would come to Ly Nam De, which marked the eastern wall of the later, Nguyen citadel. When this new east wall of the Nguyen citadel was built after Hue became capital in 1802, further west from the old citadel wall, land was freed up for building. So the streets here are relatively new, nineteenth century.

Continuing along Hang Ga, at the corner of Hang Vai, bamboo is stacked as a building material beside a flower shop where bouquets are being assembled for waiting clients to carry off, tucked under their arms on their motorbikes. I turn right into Hang Su, then left into Hang But, where I discover a street of smart new town houses. At the end of Hang But, turning right into Thuoc Bac leads me south to . . .

HANG THIEC

The noisiest street in town – and that's saying something in the Old Quarter. Hang Thiec (Tinsmith) Street originally made oil lamps, candlesticks, teapots and metal boxes. The tinsmiths here still work with sheet metal as well as selling mirrors and glass, a spin-off from tinsmithing, as tin was used to blacken the back of mirrors. Before glass mirrors, bronze and tin were highly polished as mirrors.

Rolls of metal screening and grills for balconies stand stacked in front of these shops. This is the street for furniture castors, door handles, all manner of metal fittings, as well as metal boxes of all sizes.

A temple dedicated to the patron founder of mirror-making originally stood at number 2 (now a workshop). At the bottom of Hang Thiec, the temple that stood at 42 Hang Non Street, was dedicated to the pioneer of tinsmithing, who brought the techniques to Vietnam in 1518.

In 1947, Hang Thiec became a battlefield. After first bombarding the street, the French advanced the following morning from Cua Dong through Hang Non and rolled into Hang

Thiec firing cannons. Their military garrisons were on the site of the old citadel, where by then the imperial palaces had been demolished and French military garrisons built. The fighting first lasted fourteen hours, the French occupying the odd side of the street. The next four nights saw continuous fighting. A plaque at number 5 commemorates the battle: 'On 7 February 1947, a unit of the Capital Military Forces killed hundreds of French troops in this street.' It does not say how many Vietnamese lost their lives.

HANG NON (HATS)
Hang Non Street (left) at the foot of Hang Thiec, was noted for making hats, ceremonial clothes for mandarins, costumes for traditional opera *(tuong)* and musical folk opera *(cheo)*. And what a variety of hats. It makes me yearn for a back-winding time machine to have walked these streets when all of these different kinds of hats – often badges of political power and profession – were worn, not so very long ago.

Rich people and high-ranking mandarins wore hats decorated with white feathers from the night heron with a gold or silver tip. Chiefs of villages wore hats made of black feathers with a tin or copper tip at the top.

Ordinary straw hats *(la gia)* were made of dried leaves, thick and thin. *Mu chao* hats were shaped like a pan. *Non linh,* soldiers' hats, were shaped like a large dish, using the bark of bamboo with a copper button on top and the wearer had to tie it on with a strap. The *nghe*e hat was round with an astonishingly wide diameter of one meter – and said to have been 58 centimeters (23 inches) thick. A smaller, inner cap of bamboo helped to hold it firmly on the head. *Non ba tam* hats were deeper. Both *nghe* and *ba lam* hats had metal 'strings', sometimes silver or gold to match the buttons on top. Dark violet strings, *quoi thao,* were made from twelve loops of long silk fringe.

So it would have been easy to distinguish a hat-wearer's social, political or professional position by the hat he wore.

To get an idea of the skills of the costume makers and the extravagance of theatrical costumes, you can still see performances of brief excerpts from traditional opera *(tuong)* around the corner at the National Tuong Theatre (51 Duong Thanh), a little further west (more of which later).

Hang Non runs into . . .

HANG QUAT (FANS)

Naturally in a hot, humid climate, fan making in Hanoi became a highly specialized traditional craft and probably lasted until electric fans hit the market. There were paper fans, thin silk fans, duck feather fans, fans made using bone frames, ivory frames and bamboo frames – and fans so delicately pierced that they shimmered like silk when the sun shown through. There were fans in the shapes of leaves and parallelograms. There were even fans for separating rice from the husks.

Today Hang Quat has completely changed its merchandise. The street is a riot of brass, red silk and gold tassels where all manner of religious paraphernalia is sold, ranging from small altars for shops to full-sized altars for temples, pagodas and ancestor worship in private houses. Statues of Buddha can be purchased along with ceremonial objects, funeral and prayer flags, gilt panels for mounting on temple pillars and wood blocks for printing prayer papers. It is one of the most colourful streets in the Old Quarter.

Banners bearing the Chinese ideograms for longevity, wealth and health hang above statues of Buddha, Confucius and various Tao deities. Especially popular are the female Buddha (Quan Yin), the goddess of mercy; the earth god (Ong Dia) and the god of money (Ong Tai). Look for two small china figures: Ong Dia holds a fan; Ong Tai holds a casket, presumably full of money. They often appear in small altars piled with fruit, incense and votive paper just inside shop entrances.

A friendly young girl sitting at a pavement cafe helps me to discover that the communal house of fan-makers, hidden away down an alley at 74 Hang Quat is now used as a private home.

The big, old-fashioned lock of the well-kept temple between 6 and 32 (sic) Hang Quat is opened by an old man, sitting at a nearby pavement cafe, who explains in a few words of French that it honours those who died during the wars from 1945 to 1975: World War II, the French Indo-Chinese War and the Vietnam War. He lights and hands me three joss sticks to plant in the urns on the altar, behind which a marble tableau lists their names – he is one of the few survivors.

The Dao temple at number 64, so-called because it was established by the people of Dao village (in Nam Dinh province), is dedicated to the goddess, Lieu Hanh, the goddess of Van Cat. According to one story, she was actually an angel, exiled to earth from heaven as punishment for having broken the cup containing the nectar of immortality. While on earth she died and in later reincarnations, one as Princess Lieu Hanh, she reappeared on earth and granted good luck to people.

In the second version, she was an exiled sixteenth century mandarin's daughter, who later became reincarnated as the earth mother goddess. Her followers perform ceremonies involving trance and possession. The ritual clothes for these ceremonies, of course, were bought on Hang Quat. Unfortunately, the temple looks to be permanently closed.

The west end of Hang Quat, Hang Dan (Wooden Bowls), also used to specialize in traditional stringed musical instruments.

> moon-shaped lute, *dan nguyet*
> 16-stringed zither, *dan tranh*
> monochord, *dan bau,* (one-stringed instrument)
> two-stringed fiddle, *dan nhi*
> large two-stringed fiddle, *dan ho*

HANG HOM AND HANG MANH

Two short streets run south off Hang Quat, Hang Hom (Lacquer) and Hang Manh (Split Bamboo Blinds). At first, Hang Hom specialized in making black trunks and boxes for storing clothes and document cases. Later, the boxes began to be painted, then in time they were lacquered. A temple at number 11 – its passageway now littered with plastic storage containers – honoured the master of painting and lacquering, Tran Lu, who died in 1540, who had taught his craft to the people of Binh Trang village. Wooden and bamboo instruments are still sold at numbers 1A, 4B and 16 Hang Hom.

In Hang Manh, a fairly recent specialty that came into existence just over a century ago, was the making of split bamboo blinds. At the end of 1938, number 1 Hang Manh, then a barber shop, was the secret headquarters of the Hanoi Communist Party. Hang Manh is now lined with paint shops, but shops at numbers 1, 3 and 13 keep the tradition of selling bamboo blinds. Turning left into . . .

HANG GAI

Both Hang Hom and Hang Manh run into Hanoi's luxury shopping street, Hang Gai, known to foreigners as Silk Street, shop after shop of dazzling colours. Silk is a relatively recent development in Hang Gai. In the fifteenth century this street sold rope and jute products.

From the nineteenth century, wood block printing came to Hang Gai. Printing had appeared in Vietnam as early as the twelfth century. In the Ly dynasty, a Buddhist monk named Tin Hoc (who died in 1190) had carved wood blocks to print Buddhist scriptures.

Much later in 1459, Luc Nhu Hoc went to China and learnt woodblock printing. He came back and taught his craft to his native village (in Hai Duong Province), where a communal house was set up honouring him as the founder of woodblock printing. There is still in existence a book in demotic Vietnamese script, *Truyen Ky Man Luc,* printed in 1680.

When woodblock printing came to Hang Gai in the nineteenth century, at first the books printed here were mostly traditional medical treatises and folk stories as well as a few 'popular' works such as the Confucian classics, *The Tale of Kieu* and *A Woman Baccalaureate Phan Tran.*

The Ngo Tu Ha printing house at number 101 (now selling baby clothes) was a print shop extending to Hang Hanh Street. Some thick history books required an entire room to hold the wooden engraving blocks. Houses that stored the wood blocks later became known as publishers.

Books were sold to itinerate vendors, mostly women peasants, who between harvest and planting, went around peddling farm products as well as buying up old books from families living in the countryside. These old books would be exchanged for new books in Hang Gai, put into baskets dangling from shoulder poles and carried back to rural markets to sell – primitive distribution.

When the French arrived, the houses at numbers 80-82 (now a souvenir shop and the Green Palm Gallery) became the first French embassy in Hanoi. When the Nguyen dynasty in Hue appointed a mandarin, Nguyen Trong Hop, as governor of the North, he set up headquarters at number 79 and lived at number 83 (now a jewellery shop), opposite the Residence de France.

It was the French ambassador who first brought rickshaws to Hanoi from Japan. From general to mandarin and of course, the French, everyone travelled by rickshaw, in those days pulled by a man on foot.

An old man sitting in front of the jewellery shop at number 83 tells me that the small temple next door under a fig tree is three hundred years old and writes its name: Dinh Co Vu. Vietnamese scholar, Huu Ngoc, the writer from whose works much of the historical background and translations for this book have been drawn, grew up as a child in Hang Gai and remembers going there many times with his father, who was president of the council of notables of Co Vu village. The temple was, in fact, the communal house *(dinh)* of Co Vu village at the back of which was a print shop.

Among Huu Ngoc's childhood memories are the mid-autumn children's festivals, when the street was a child's delight, hung with bright lanterns in the shape of lion heads, rabbits, toads, fish and dragons. For a time during the resistance against the French, they controlled the odd numbered side of the street; the Vietnamese controlled the even numbered side.

Slowly, more shops began to appear: stationery shops, hat shops, an optician. These days, Hang Gai is a silk shopper's paradise: shimmering scarves and stoles, finely tailored men's and women's clothes, heavily embroidered and sequined evening gowns, handbags, silk bed throws. Choose your silk – nubbly raw silk, thick heavy silk, finely patterned or plain, a kaleidoscope of deep, rich colours or a selection of subtle pale pastels. If it's not hanging on a rack, it will be tailored to your measurements and requirements in twenty-four to forty-eight hours (best to have Western tailoring copied). From Hang Gai, it is only a few steps along Luang Van Can (turn right) to Hoan Kiem and a rewarding cup of tea, coffee or ice cream at Thuy Ta, overlooking the lake.

ARRIVAL OF THE FRENCH

He who sows the wind will reap the whirlwind
– Vietnamese proverb

To set the historical stage for the arrival of the French, when the Nguyen dynasty seized power in 1802 and shifted the capital to Hue, the importance of Thang Long suddenly shrank to that of an ignominious provincial capital – with a governor appointed by Hue. In 1805, the second Nguyen emperor, Minh Mang, even went so far as to tear down Thang Long's citadel and to replace it with his own smaller, fortress-style citadel to bring home to the Hanoians exactly where power lay. In the south, Catholic uprisings in Saigon against the Nguyens in 1833 were brutally put down by Minh Mang, leaving a festering of ill will.

From the early nineteenth century both France and England had coveted opening the lucrative Chinese market. Following the Opium Wars in 1842 in China, the British obtained trading rights, 'favoured nation' status in a treaty of 1857. The thinking of the French must have gone something like this. By establishing a foothold in South East Asia, by controlling the deltas of the Red river (Hong Song) in the north and the Mekong river in the south, whose sources arose in China, French traders would be able to penetrate deep into China along these rivers.

However, in an early expedition up the Mekong led by Francis Garnier and Daudart de Lagnee, the shallow rapids of southern Laos known as the Four Thousand Islands, proved an insurmountable obstacle. Not to be deterred, the French set to and built a short railway alongside the rapids and a railway bridge over the river a bit upstream. Today, nothing remains of this optimistic tropical misadventure but a rusty engine on an isolated length of track, stranded in a Lao village. In terms of building it – think the Burma Railway.

The Mekong in the south having proved un-navigable for heavy shipping, France decided to take Tonkin, the north of Vietnam, in order to gain access to China up the Red river.

To thread our way through the labyrinthine chronology of France's creeping advancement into Indo-China, although it had been with French military support that the Nguyens came to power in 1802, the second Nguyen emperor, Minh Mang, and the third and fourth Nguyen emperors, Thieu Tri and Tu Duc, had become quite hostile to Western French influence, particularly to Catholicism, which they considered a foreign threat to Confucianism. Using Tu Duc's persecution of French priests as a pretext, the French attacked Tourane (also called Turon, now Danang) Harbour in 1858, leaving the Nguyen emperor little choice but to grant the port of Tourane to the French as a trading concession. The following year on 17 July 1859, the French took Saigon militarily, possibly made easier by Saigon still feeling rankled over Ming Mang's viciousness in putting down an earlier Catholic insurrection.

The treaty of 1864 recognized French control over three cities and provinces in the south: Saigon, My Tho and Bien Hoa. That same year, the students who were to have sat the preliminary mandarin examinations in Hanoi were so incensed by what they saw as Hue's acquiescence to the French that they held a ceremony in the Temple of Literature, after which they refused to sit the examinations and made a protest march around Hoan Kiem lake, declaring their intention to go south and join the armed resistance against the French.

In 1867, French repression of the resistance movement in the south resulted in French occupation of a further three cities and their provinces in the Mekong delta: Vinh Long, Ha Tien and Chao Doc. Then on 20 November 1873, with a small expeditionary force of fewer than two hundred men, Francis Garnier captured Hanoi's citadel. If a small expeditionary force could take Hanoi's citadel, Emperor Tu Duc realized that he had little chance against a full French army. On 15 March 1874, he agreed to a treaty, still recognizing the independence of Annam (central Vietnam), but opening the Red river in the north to international commerce.

Much to the chagrin of Hanoi, the imperial court in Hue continued to conduct peaceful negotiations with the French instead as they saw it, of resisting militarily. Eventually, in exchange for returning the now empty citadel in Hanoi, the French were given a land concession to install a Navy Cantonment a bit south of Hoan Kiem lake along the Red river, near and beyond where Hanoi's History Museum now stands.

This land was created by filling in ponds between Hoan Kiem lake and the Red river. In this area, the French built functional military quarters surrounded by open verandas.

In 1882, Hanoi's citadel fell to the French once again, this time to Henri Riviere, this time for the last time. Hanoi's defeated governor, Hoang Dieu, committed suicide in despair. Only one year later, armed French troops started to build the road between the citadel and the Naval Concession east of Hoan Kiem.

Following the death of Emperor Tu Duc in July of 1883, the French forced Tu Duc's successor, Hiep Hoa, to sign the first Convention of Protectorate. It was ratified, 6 June 1884, by the Treaty of Patenôtre (named after the negotiator), which relinquished sovereignty over all three regions: Cochin in the South, Annam in Central and Tonkin in North Vietnam. Hanoi, belonging to Tonkin, fell under the French Protectorate.

From that moment on, Vietnamese emperors in Hue – despite occasional resistance – were reduced to puppets and their mandarins were forced to follow French orders. This treaty also enlarged the French concession to include the area south and west of Hoan Kiem Lake, the beginnings of the French Quarter; the Vietnamese called it the Westerners' Quarter.

In 1885, inside Hanoi's citadel walls – where royal palaces and mandarin buildings had once stood – the French began building military quarters, and in 1887, announced their Indo-Chinese Union consisting of Cochin, Annam, Tonkin and Cambodia. Laos was added in 1894.

After a short war, also in 1887, the French obtained a trade agreement with China. The frontier between the two countries was marked and China relinquished any remnant of sovereignty remaining over Vietnam as a vassal state. Permission to build a railway to the Chinese frontier was also granted. The wily General de Negrier, commander of the French army, immediately after his victorious battle, demanded that a sign be painted in Chinese and affixed to the Friendly Gate reading: 'Borders are not protected by stone walls, but by the enforcement of treaties.'

The borders agreed in the Treaty of Tianjin remain unchanged to this day, either by the establishment of the Republic of China in 1911, or later, when Vietnam gained independence from the French. The only time a border question has arisen was during the sixteen-day skirmish between Vietnam and China in 1979 when

China set out 'to teach Vietnam a lesson,' following Vietnam's defeat of the Chinese-supported Pol Pot regime in Cambodia. In fact, it was the battle-hardened Vietnamese who sent the Chinese scurrying, according to Vietnamese sources, leaving an estimated twenty thousand Chinese dead in just over two weeks.

The Indo-Chinese Union proclaimed by the French in 1887 may have ended the legal existence of independent Vietnam, but active resistance continued in various parts of the country right up to World War II and then, of course, afterwards in the French Indo-Chinese War.

In Hanoi, the first large-scale French construction projects began with the arrival of the first French governors in the 1880s. From 1887, the French undertook to plan, build and modernize Hanoi in the image of a French city of the Third Republic with the same vigour and expedience with which they had pursued their development of the Indo-Chinese Union (Cochin, Annam, Tonkin, Cambodia and Laos).

To link the southern provinces, they succeeded in the not inconsiderable feat of building a narrow-gauge railway, 1,036 miles (1,657 km) long, from the Chinese border through Hanoi, along the coastal plain to Saigon – the track is still used. In Hanoi, a railway bridge named for the French governor, Paul Doumer, was built over the Red river by French engineers. It has now been renamed Long Bien bridge and despite repeated American bombings and subsequent repairs, remains open to non-motorized and railway traffic.

Very early on, the French, viewing Hanoi's muddle of clay and brick, wood and thatch huts, cluttering a thicket of narrow lanes, each entered through a gate, closed and guarded at night, set out to create streets in the Western sense of the word.

In the area south and west of Hoan Kiem lake, the homes and shops of locals were cleared to make way for broad, paved boulevards along which plane trees and *hoa sua* (milk trees) were planted for shade.

In the Old Quarter, rivers and ponds were filled in to prevent malaria and to provide more building land. Water pipes were laid and sewers dug. At first there were gas street lamps. Later, electricity lines were strung up for the first time, a tramway was built, running on quiet rubber wheels, the rubber naturally supplied by French-owned rubber plantations.

The main street of the new French Quarter was Trang Tien, then called Rue Paul Bert, in honour of the French Resident General of Tonkin appointed in 1886 – he whose statue stood in what is now Ly Thai To park. Built on land to the east, gained by filling in ponds between Hoan Kiem lake and the Red river, Rue Paul Bert was known for an imposing department store, the *Grands Magasins Reunis,* as well as for cafes with live music, luxury hotels and restaurants, smart cinemas and of course, later for the opera.

South and parallel to Rue Paul Bert, came three more boulevards running east-west: Rollandes, now Hai Ba Trung; Carreau, now Ly Thuong Kiet and Gambetta, named after the French Prime Minister, Leon Gambetta (1838-1882), now Tran Hung Dao. Streets of the French Quarter were laid out in a grid, each square parcel of land allotted to a French officer and his family for their private villa, surrounded by a garden. The grandness of the villa depended upon the social status and wealth of the owner, who often worked with his architect on the design.

Naturally, architectural styles reflected nostalgia for France because French officials and their wives, coming to far-away Indo-China, clearly preferred to live in houses that reminded them familiarly of home. Villa styles echoed Paris, northern, central and southern France, as long as the transplanted styles worked in Hanoi's constantly damp, monsoon climate.

Northern France contributed such characteristics as tall, grand villas with multifaceted steep roofs (so that snow could slide off) and high turrets to afford panoramic views of the surrounding countryside. At first, decoration was simple, rectangles or hexagrams marking the corners of the buildings.

From central France came less steep roofs, windows divided into many small panes and more delicate wall decorations, especially around the windows of second-floor balconies or in arches. From the mountainous regions came towers and gazebos.

From the south of France and the shores of the Mediterranean came flat roofs or roofs at a slight angle with slate or tile roofs to deflect the sun, atriums and courtyards in front, as well as the use of natural, unfinished materials in asymmetrical facades.

A distinguishing characteristic of southern-style houses were the canopies, extending from the entrances of buildings to meet the visitor. Apart from the canopies one sees on several French colonial buildings, few in this southern style were built in Hanoi as they didn't work well in the city's harsh, humid climate.

Early on, all of Hanoi's new streets were numbered, more than three hundred of them. Gradually, the numbers were replaced by the names of French notables, particularly generals and former governors of Indo-China: Boulevard Felix Faure, honouring the president of the French Republic (1895-1899); Boulevard de l'Admiral Courbet; Rue Henri-Riviere, who had captured the citadel; Rue General Leclanger; Rue Capitaine Labrousse. Streets having Vietnamese names were changed to French names. Well, Indo-China was now a little bit of France in the tropics, although to put it mildly, the Vietnamese never saw it quite that way.

What a contrast the lovely trees and lavish, spacious villas along these new streets must have presented to the Vietnamese living in the Old Quarter's narrow, compact, almost treeless lanes, heaving with Vietnamese families living almost on top of one another. The French Quarter gradually crept northward on both sides of Hoan Kiem Lake, virtually to the southern edge of the Thirty-Six Streets along the north bank of the lake.

To the west, it extended even beyond the citadel, stopped only in the north by West Lake. It is little wonder that the Vietnamese hated the them so much. As well as having seized political control, the French had destroyed homes and pagodas and displaced families. Moreover, the Vietnamese people were forced to pay heavy taxes to support all this ambitious construction of infrastructure.

In the second stage of urban development, French government administration buildings began to be built. The architect, Auguste-Henri Vildieu, head of Civil Construction in Indo-China (1892-1906), as designer for a colonial regime anxious to assert its power, renounced the utilitarianism of the 1880s and instead, relied upon the solidity and decorative vocabulary of Neo-Classical architecture to command the attention and respect of the Vietnamese masses. Buildings constructed under his regime reflect his rather austere if grand taste, a style almost devoid of ostentatious decoration, modelled to suit a hot humid climate: large mullioned windows to provide airflow with protective protruding frames, roofs of slate or tile. In 1896-97, the French finally razed what little remained of

Emperor Gia Long's Vauban-style citadel to make way for their own military garrisons.

Vildieu oversaw the design and building of numerous administrative buildings – a court, a customs house, a hospital, hotels and inevitably, a prison – in addition to schools, lycees, colleges and universities in styles reflecting regional French and the Neo-Classicism of the contemporary Third Republic.

In 1923 Ernest Hebrard took up his duties in Hanoi in Central Services of Urban Planning and Architecture. He was the architect, perhaps more than any other, who created the eclectic style incorporating architectural features of indigenous Vietnamese, Chinese and Khmer royal and religious architecture, adapting them to large-scale French designs, which eventually became known as Indo-Chinese style. It had been his intention to bring all the administration buildings into one area beyond the Governor General's palace to the west of the citadel, south of West Lake. Alas, his vision required too much capital just at a time when the French economy was weak. Nevertheless, his plans remained the official reference well into the 1940s.

French influence extended well beyond architecture – to food, art, music, literature, above all, to education. Apart from the *lycees,* a School of Fine Arts, teaching Western style art, music and architecture was opened as well as Colleges of Law and Medicine. French scholars took an intense interest in Vietnamese culture, establishing *l'Ecole Française d'Extrême Orient* (the French School of the Far East).

In 1910, by abolishing the Chinese based *chu nom* writing – inaccessible to the French – in favour of the Romanized script, *quoc ngu,* and by ending the mandarin examinations in 1919, the French barred young Vietnamese scholars from their birthright to traditional Vietnamese education and scholarship – sharply cutting off the younger generation from their cultural roots in Vietnamese literature and history. But the Vietnamese, their nationalism and cultural identity galvanized by the bitter memory of a millennium of suffering under the yoke of Chinese imperialism, remained a seething foment of active resistance throughout the entire French period.

By the early twentieth century, the Meiji of Japan was the only successful model of an independent state maintaining an imperial system in Asia. In Vietnam, a traditional patriotic scholar, having witnessed the disintegration of Vietnam's imperial system, set up a study-abroad programme called Eastbound Exodus, which allowed young Vietnamese to be sent to Tokyo for political and military training – amazing that he got away with it under the French.

Another Vietnamese, Phan Chao Trinh, advocated a more radical approach – creating democracy through widespread education for all. In the year the Chinese Manchu empire collapsed (1911), a young man steeped in Trinh's extremist philosophy, set sail for Marseilles. Nguyen Tat Thanh was the son of a low-grade mandarin, who had been dismissed for his unacceptable views. In the West, young Thanh did any menial job going to support himself. He worked and studied in Paris, London, New York and finally after 1923, in Moscow. In 1942, he recognized that the time was imminent to make a bid for his country's independence. It was then that he took his final of some fifty aliases: Nguyen the Patriot, Ho Chi Minh.

Much of Hanoi's charm lies in the legacy of its old tree-lined French avenues; the elegant French-built government buildings, now museums or ministries; the splendid restored opera house; the renovated Metropole Hotel; the many elegant villas and it must be admitted, even the beauty and magic of Hoan Kiem lake, which before the French arrived, was encircled by muddy banks and street-less wood and thatch villages, temples and pagodas.

Under the French, Hanoi never quite approached either Shanghai or Hong Kong in importance as a trade centre. Steamers may have plied the Red river between Hanoi and Haiphong, but Hanoi lacked a really deep harbour – the Red river proved un-navigable into the heart of China.

Following their defeat at Dien Bien Phu, as soon as the French left Hanoi in 1954, the Vietnamese took over the French Quarter as well as the French-built government buildings.

With independence following the Vietnam War in 1975, a collective feeling arose in Vietnam concerning the need to preserve Hanoi's architectural heritage, not only the Thirty-Six Streets and the citadel area, but the French Quarter. For a country struggling in the aftermath of war – three almost consecutive wars – so much needed to be done, so quickly and with no money. Other more urgent needs took priority. So the Vietnamese made do with what they had, leased the grandest villas to foreign governments for embassies or offices and sub-divided many villas for multiple-occupancy, tacking shops on the front. This benign neglect meant the survival of much of Vietnam's French colonial architectural heritage, rather than demolition and new buildings – until the past ten years.

To a Western town planner, Hanoi's Old Quarter of Thirty-Six Streets still might appear to be a tangled warren of electricity and telephone wires (many of them illegally tapping into the supply), with a jumble of cubical excretions on roofs whenever a family has had enough money to add another room or a temple to their ancestors. Many of these old houses were overcrowded – they still are – and lacked even minimal sanitation. When people could afford to, families have literally torn down their old family homes and replaced them with five and six-storey houses or mini-hotels with little thought of preservation – often moving elsewhere.

But for the past few years, there has been a strong feeling that Hanoi's architectural legacy, French villas as well as the old tube houses in the Thirty-Six Streets, those that remain, must be preserved as Vietnam's heritage.

THE FRENCH COLONIAL LEGACY

The mandarin passes by, the people remain
– Vietnamese proverb

Once established, having installed modern infrastructure and imposed stately government buildings, as their colonial commercial adventure developed and endured, the French lived graciously in Hanoi. Their elaborate villas and mansions bear witness to their status as masters. Servants did the menial tasks and colonial life became a fashionable social whirl of cafes and restaurants; shopping, parties and dances; concerts, the theatre and latterly, the cinema; punctuated by regular visits to the races, *le Club Sportif* and casino, which doubled as an unofficial club.

French architecture in Hanoi represents a wide spectrum of styles, harking backwards to the classicism of the Third Republic and forward to *beaux arts, art deco* and the modernism of the first half of the twentieth century, including the hybrid Indo-Chinese style that developed here.

Hanoi's finest landmarks of colonial architecture are concentrated in two main areas. Suppose we stroll round the centre of the city to the east and south of Hoan Kiem Lake, possibly dividing this meander into two strolls – or you might prefer to hire a cyclo. The third cluster of grand official buildings around Ba Dinh Square needs a taxi or a motorbike taxi *(xe om)*.

STATE BANK OF VIETNAM
(Ho Chu Tich Song Mai Trong Su Nghiep Cua Chung)

Starting from Hoan Kiem lake at the back of Ly Thai To park, lording it over the junction where Ngo Quyen and Ly Thai To Streets cross, stands the rather pompous former *Banque d'Indochine*. This late, rather weighty *art deco* edifice, completed in 1930, was designed by George-Andre Trouve, a young architect straight out of the School of Fine Arts in Paris.

Looking more like a monument or a mausoleum than a bank with its massive unadorned columns and militant rows of recessed windows, the entry porch under a tiered, heavy-lidded, circular flattened cupola, repeats the theme of bulky, plain-faced columns. With luck, the guard may let you peek inside at what was the enormous banking hall.

Here the young architect excelled himself. As it was out of the question in such a hot, humid climate to use direct sunlight to provide good lighting for the bank clerks, he cleverly invented a system of opaque domes, light filtering through twenty 'lanterns' to provide diffuse overhead lighting.

If 1930s *art deco* is not quite your idea of French colonial architecture, the next example is in astonishing contrast . . .

GOVERNMENT GUEST HOUSE *(Nha Khach Chinh Phu)*

Just around the corner (right) at 12 Ngo Quyen, the former French *Palais du Gouvernement Général* is now used as the Government Guest House. Clearly, this building was designed on a grand scale to impress the Vietnamese and to reflect the power of France. It must be said that the new French government administration buildings literally dwarfed the scale of Vietnamese architecture of the period.

On one occasion at a reception for the penultimate emperor, Khai Dinh, held in this very building, a Vietnamese journalist is said to have remarked, 'The lay ceremony of Hue, set in its own suitable surroundings, is grand and impressive, whereas here, it seems mean and puny and extravagant.'

Once inside the elaborate wrought-iron gates and courtyard, apart from the ochre colour and green-shuttered windows, this Neo-Classical building might well be a chateau lifted from Napoleonic France. A steep, tiled roof rises above the central entrance; plaster-work medallions festoon the facade, the corners marked by Ionic pilasters, eloquently stating in architectural terms the grandeur of France's ambitions for Indo-China.

A sweeping ornamental, central staircase opens on the raised ground floor to a vast entrance foyer, leading in turn to a grand circular salon looking out over the gardens. French administration offices occupied the wings of the raised ground floor; the two upper floors were devoted to accommodation for the governor. It was designed by Charles Lichenfelder under Auguste-Henri Vildieu, head of Civil Construction in Indo-China (1892-1906) and completed in 1907.

Continuing along Ngo Quyen is one of Hanoi's oldest and grandest hotels.

HOTEL SOFITEL METROPOLE

The old Metropole Hotel with its classic Citroens parked out in front, was Hanoi's first luxury hotel. In it heydays it played host to moustachioed planters, colonial administrators and smart French army officers and their ladies. In the twenties, jazz and the Charleston became the rage at the nightly dances. Completed in 1901, its illustrious visitors' book holds the names of Somerset Maugham, Noel Coward and Graham Green – Charlie Chaplin spent his honeymoon at the Metropole – along with numerous heads of state, European royalty, and later, film stars such as Catherine Deneuve, Jane Fonda (while she did her controversial broadcasts), Michael Cain (filming *The Quiet American),* even Mick Jagger and Robert De Niro. It seems that nearly everyone of any note has stayed there, except perhaps you and me.

The traditional Neo-Classical facade remains, now painted white (I suspect it was originally ochre). The arched, green-shuttered windows and balustrade balconies look out towards the former *Hôtel du Coq* opposite, now the Ministry of Labour, War Wounded and Social Affairs.

In the restoration by the Sofitel group, the interior has been renovated and updated in the spirit of a luxurious traditional hotel – dark wood panelling, antique-style oriental furniture, ceiling fans (ornamental), blue and white ceramics of the period. The dark-stained wooden fretwork that frames the square atrium, opening through several floors, is particularly fine and might well be a replication or the original. Strolling through the lobby to the bar, a good place for a lemonade, noting the old photographs of Hanoi as I go, I leave from the back of the building and turn right into Ly Thai To Street, then take a sharp left into Trang Tien at the far side of the triangular park beside the opera house. A few steps along on the right at the corner of Pham Ngu Lao is . . .

HISTORY MUSEUM *(Bao Tang Lich Su)*

The building, formerly the Louis-Finot Museum, was associated with *l'Ecole Française d'Extrême Orient,* a scholarly organization concerned with archaeological, historical and ethnological research. During the French period, this organization fought to preserve and in some cases to restore Vietnamese temples and pagodas, as well as Vietnam's archaeological heritage in the form of the brick Cham temples and stone sculpture in the south.

The museum was the masterpiece of architect Ernest Hebrard, winner of the *Prix de Rome* in 1904, who was responsible for several fine buildings during the colonial era, borrowing from the repertoire of Chinese, Vietnamese and Khmer traditional architecture. Here, he adopted a whimsical mixture of classical French, and Vietnamese community house *(dinh)* and pagoda *(chua)* styles, the Asian architectural features in keeping with the building's original use and now, its current function.

Hebrard, more than any other architect, created what has come to be known as the eclectic Indo-Chinese style architecture.

The central core of the building is octagonal, from which the galleries branch out like streets from a roundabout. The wide, overhanging double tile roofs over the external galleries form the dominant feature, echoing domestic architecture, the deep eaves providing shade for the rooms within. The criss-crossed supporting beams in the style of temple architecture, give the external galleries the impression that the tile roofs are actually floating. Along the galleries, by employing slim, round, double columns to resemble wooden posts, Hebrard was able to use brick and plaster in a way common to vernacular architecture.

Charles Batteur, architect and professor at *l'Ecole des Beaux Arts,* took charge of the detail of the numerous drawings and acted as site manager. Held up by over-running its budget, the building was not completed finally until 1931.

Exhibits in the History Museum are arranged chronologically, starting on the ground floor, with Bronze Age drums of the Dong Son culture and jewellery of the Sa Huynh culture, Cham pottery and sculpture, on through lacquered Buddhist statues, pale green celadon ceramics and a few of the wooden stakes from the fifteenth-century battle victory of the Bach Dang river when military hero Le Loi of the restored sword defeated the Chinese.

Upstairs are a handful of early Cham statues from central and south Vietnam, which slightly pre-dated Angkor in Cambodia. Also upstairs are exhibits relating to the last dynasty, the Nguyen – the last emperor abdicated as recently as 1945: embroidered silks, gilt and inlaid ivory furniture, watercolours of Vietnam's last imperial court and a photograph of Hue's citadel in 1932 – before the bombings of World War II and the Vietnam War.

To see the building that Hebrard used as his artistic laboratory, his first in Hanoi, we need to have a look at the University of Indo-China. But first, let's cross the street and take a sharp left from the History Museum to the entrance of . . .

MUSEUM OF THE REVOLUTION *(Bao Tang Cach Mang)*

Hardly surprisingly, one of the first public buildings completed by the French was the customs house (1903), situated originally on the former Quay Clemenceau, facing the Red river. Recalling that a good part of the resources of the colony came from taxes on the import and export of merchandise, including taxes on salt, alcohol and opium, this would have been an important building. The style of architecture is similar to numerous public buildings designed by architect Henri Vildieu. The entrance is topped by a moulded arch, its minimal decoration based on a play of tall rectangular windows separated by pilasters.

Inside are displays of numerous documents from the Vietnamese movement for independence, a room dedicated to the life of Ho Chi Minh and other rooms tracing the Vietnam War.

Retracing my steps round the corner into Trang Tien, I walk back to what these days is known prosaically as the municipal theatre, although even taxi drivers still call it the Opera.

THE MUNICIPAL THEATRE *(No Hat Lon)*

The Opera is the building that many consider to be the golden glory of French architectural achievement in Hanoi and I must admit, my favourite French colonial building. Modelled on Charles Garnier's *Opéra de Paris* in flamboyant Neo-Baroque style, the Opera was designed by Francois Lagisquet and completed in 1911, according to Vietnamese sources – or 1914, if you believe French art historians. In its time, it was the only European style opera house east of Cairo.

From afar, the rectangular porticos at two levels of this golden vision are supported by tall Ionic columns, behind which is a wide central balcony terrace at the upper level. The roof cornice is joyously festooned with statues of griffons.

When I was shown through the building for the first time in 1997 by the Vietnamese architect in charge of its restoration, Dr Prof Hoang Dao Kinh, he was immensely proud that a poor country like Vietnam had found the fourteen million US dollars 'to build a temple to the arts for all the people.' Closely following the original plans, but installing air-conditioning and heating, he was determined to remain faithful to the fabric of the original.

All of the new materials were to come from Vietnam, the slates from Sin Ho, the clay chimney pots from Nha Trang. Italians had supervised the relaying of the mosaic floor in the foyer and French artists had seen to the ornamental details of its fine Corinthian columns in the red-plush auditorium that holds up to eight hundred.

'It may have been designed by a French architect, but it was built by Vietnamese hands. The Vietnamese are very fine craftsmen.' He led me up the grand central staircase to the first floor foyer and at first I thought he was pointing to the gracefully curved wooden frames of the *art deco* mirrors, but no, he was pointing to the walls.

'There were many bullet holes here, many people died, both French and Vietnamese.'

Throughout the French Indo-Chinese War and later, during the Vietnam War, the building was left to decay. Nevertheless on 19 August 1945, following the surrender of the Japanese, Ho Chi Minh's Revolutionary Committee rushed to the balcony of the *Opera,* unfurled their banners and declared the establishment of the independent Socialist Republic of Vietnam.

The mirrored salon is one of the most elegant and charming opera foyers I know, even compared to some of the great opera houses of Europe. To visit the glorious interior of the Opera with its marble staircases, crystal chandeliers and gold paintwork, watch Vietnam News for announcements of concerts, often featuring high standard soloists from abroad.

With my back to the opera, I cross the open junction to Trang Tien Street, directly in front of the *Opera.* On the corner to the left is the domed building that formerly housed an up-market French department store, *Grands magazins reunis,* the name of each department set in mosaic above an arched window. The building now houses the Hanoi Stock Exchange. I walk a few steps along Trang Tien, then turn and look back. This is the most impressive view of the *Opera.* Trang Tien was the chic shopping street during the French era and it is still lined with art galleries, booksellers and shops selling beautiful lacquer and embroidered table and bed linen. (Stop now, if you are tired).

Returning to the *Opera,* I turn south (right) into Ngo Quyen, which has by now metamorphosed into Le Thanh Tong.

UNIVERSITY OF HANOI *(Ho Chu Tich)*

On the left at 19 Le Thanh Tong, the former *Université d'Indochine,* completed in 1927, is now part of Hanoi University. When Ernest Hebrard first arrived in Hanoi in 1923, his colleagues, Charles Lacollonge, chief of service and his assistant, Paul Sabrie, had already sent a proposal, had it approved by the Governor General and the foundations had been laid for the new university building.

Notwithstanding, riding on his *Prix de Rome,* Hebrard imposed his authority upon the team, stopped construction and ordered the team to research Asian architectural features. At this time, he looked towards models of Asian empire, beginning with the most prestigious of that era, the imperial palaces of the Forbidden City of Beijing.

As a result, a timid Sinization of the building took place: the flared canopy of the drum of the cupola, the double roofs over the porch and a lantern reflecting the curves of the crown of a stupa. The squared angularity of the open parapet railings are an exact copy of those in China.

Nevertheless, the revised drawings still carried more than a trace of the initial design inspired by eighteenth century France: the height of reception spaces, the immense dome and its lantern, the arches, the wide corridors and the classical facade. Yet the design also shows Hebrard's intense determination, having become officially director of Central Service of Architecture and Urbanism in 1923, to create what would later become known as the *style d'Indochine.*

Just opposite the university is Ly Thong Kiet. Two city blocks along this street, at the corner I slip into the former Splendid Hotel for a look at the romantic, indeed splendid, wooden stairway. Renamed the Ba Trieu Hotel, it was built by the French in the thirties (alas, no longer there).

Despite the sudden intrusion of modern high-rise buildings here and there, the east-west streets of this quarter still retain a good many old French villas.

Continuing along Ly Thong Kiet, opposite the Melia Hotel at number 59 is a grand villa, now premises of the Vietnam Atomic Energy Commission; the *art deco* villas at numbers 65 and 65A are now occupied by the Cuban Embassy.

Just near here on the left, is a narrow lane leading to a market selling fruit and vegetables and if you look for it, 'sides' of dog meat. It is called the 19th December Market – the date the Vietnamese Revolution officially began.

During 1946-47, this lane was used to bury dead resistance fighters. Their bodies have now been moved, but it is said that the stall keepers still burn incense in their memory.

SUPREME COURT *(Tao An Nhyan Dan)*

This ochre building served as the French *Palais de Justice;* it now serves as the Vietnamese Supreme Court. It was designed by Auguste-Henri Vildieu (1900-1906), who shamelessly drew inspiration from the Neo-Classical *Palais du Justice* in Paris, designed by Louis Duc (1857-1868).

From the street, it is not at all evident that the building is in the shape of an inverted 'T'. Every feature is symmetrical, exactly balanced – as in justice, as in Confucianism. The raised ground floor is reached by a bifurcated staircase.

Under a mansard roof, three elegant cornices bind the two tiers of mullioned windows of the building, separated by fluted columns. Conveniently close to the court, the next street is dolefully named after the prison . . .

HOA LO PRISON *(Nha Thu Hoa Lo)*

Euphemistically called by the French, the *Maison Centrale,* this is another infamous hostelry, known to American GIs as the Hanoi Hilton. Hoa Lo Prison, designed by Auguste-Henri Vildieu and built by the French in 1899 – even before the Customs House – was later used as a prison by the Vietnamese. Originally much larger and planned to hold four hundred fifty prisoners, records show that at one time in the thirties under the French, it held nearly 2,000 in what must have been desperately cramped and miserable conditions. Many Vietnamese nationalist leaders were incarcerated here, no fewer than five future general secretaries of the Vietnamese Communist Party and later, numerous American POWs. One of them, Pete Peterson, later became the first American ambassador to Vietnam in 1995. John McCain was also imprisoned here. It was used as a prison right up to 1994.

When the tower and hotel were built next door, only a very small portion of the prison was retained as a museum, preserving a few cells, their rusty shackles and instruments of torture. Among them is a guillotine, used to behead Vietnamese resistance fighters during the colonial period. Considered a swift, compassionate means of execution by the French, the guillotine was used in France until 1977!

Continuing along Ly Thuong Kiet, note the beautiful old villas at number 66, residence of the Australian ambassador; number 88, the Ministry of Trade and number 72, the extraordinarily angular UNDP building.

At the end of Ly Thuong Kiet, to the left is Hanoi's railway station. The entrance was destroyed by American bombs and has been replaced by incongruous modernity. But the rest of the building bears the hallmarks of French colonial style: ochre stucco walls, black-shuttered rectangular windows.

One street further south is Tran Hung Dao – yes, named after the general who saw off the Mongols in the thirteenth century. Extending an entire city block, number 85 on the left corner, is another fine example of French Neo-Classical architecture, now the Ministries of Labour and Transport. Fine colonial buildings now house the Immigration Office at number 89, Police Headquarters at number 87 and several grand villas have been turned into embassies: the Norwegian Embassy at number 41, the

Indian Embassy at number 58, the French Embassy (much rebuilt and enlarged) at number 53 and the Cambodian Embassy at the corner of Tran Hung Dao and Ngo Quyen.

FRENCH COLONIAL BUIDINGS, BA DINH SQUARE

To reach the cluster of official buildings around Ba Dinh Square, wheeled transport of one sort or another is required – this is too far for cyclos – and as the buildings are widely spaced out, it's either a taxi or for better visibility, a motorbike taxi *(xe om)*.

From the south end of Hoan Kiem lake travel along Pho Trang Thi, then take a diagonal right, north-west into Dien Bien Phu. Many of the elegant French villas along this lovely old tree-lined boulevard have been turned into embassies: the Danish Embassy as number 19, the Malaysian Embassy at number 43, the German Embassy and Residence at number 40 and the Swiss Embassy at number 49.

HEXAGONAL FLAG TOWER *(Cot Co)*

The flag tower is certainly not a French colonial structure, but as one of only two remaining relics from Nguyen Emperor Gia Long's nineteenth-century citadel (1812), it is well worth a detour, not only for its historical interest, but especially for the view from the top, if the tower is open. In fact, it is courtesy of the French that the flag tower still stands – they found it useful as a watchtower when they demolished the Nguyen citadel.

Vietnam's flag, gold star on a red field, has flown proudly from this tower, day and night since 10 October 1954. Entrance to the flag tower is through the grounds of the Museum of Military History, littered with wrecked planes and the remnants of armaments. Inside the museum (for which you will have bought a ticket to see the flag tower) is a scale model of the battle of Dien Bien Phu and the very bicycle used by the Vietnamese to transport artillery to the decisive French-Vietnamese showdown.

The flagpole is mounted on a sturdy three-tier, square brick platform – impressive if not beautiful. If you are lucky and the tower is unlocked, from the top on a clear day you can just make out the metal arches of Long Bien bridge off to the east, or look down into what was the citadel area, now the Vietnamese army headquarters and out of bounds to visitors. Only the old north gate of the Nguyen citadel *(Cua Bac)* is on view, its brickwork heavily scarred by a French bombardment in 1882.

From Cot Co Flag Tower, go north along Dien Bien Phu to . .

BA DINH SQUARE *(Quang Truong Ba Dinh)*

This large grassy rectangle is only a small portion of the area once occupied by the ancient Ly and the later Nguyen citadels. After the defeat of the French, Ba Dinh Square became Vietnam's ceremonial parade ground, a rather friendlier Vietnamese equivalent of Red Square or Tiananmen Square.

MINISTRY OF FOREIGN AFFAIRS *(Bao Ngoai Giao)*

At the south-east corner of Ba Dinh Square stands another of Ernest Hebrand's architectural triumphs, designed for the French Ministry of Finance and completed in 1931. His characteristic oriental double-tiled roof of the hexagonal guard-house sets the Indo-Chinese mood of this three-storey building. Each window and balcony is protected from the sun by a tiled canopy in a studied use of traditional techniques in response to the climate.

Intertwining patterns that resemble woven straw are used as a wall frieze between the windows at the uppermost level. Lamps in the form of miniature pagodas light the access ramp and stylised lotus buds crown the pillars of the low wall in front of the building. Although out of context, all of these ornamental features demonstrate close attention to the Vietnamese architectural repertoire. In the space of only twenty years, the time between Henri Vildieu and Ernest Hebrand, the concept of the role of a colonial architect had changed dramatically.

CENTRAL COMMITTEE *(Uy ban Trung Uong)*

At the top of Ba Dinh Square, the former *Lycée Albert-Sarraut,* named after a governor general, was designed by the French firm, Verneuil & Gravereaud (1920). The lycée, which educated many young French students as well as elite Vietnamese, now serves as the Information Section of the Central Committee of the Communist Party. Designed on a strict symmetrical plan, alternating interior courtyards, classrooms and accommodation for students, the style of this building marks the end of European classicism in Indo-China, introducing a style of ornamentation tinged with *art nouveau.*

Inside, the honour of decorating the vestibule and the stairway of honour was assigned in 1933 to the painter, Jos Ponchin, confirming the cultural mind-set to which, presumably, the *lycée* at that time subscribed. In his work the artist, winner of the *Prix de l'Indochine,* represents France bringing the benefits of civilization to Indo-China. I can't help wondering, mischievously, if Ponchin's mural was painted over when the building was taken over by the Central Committee of the Communist Party (I am not allowed inside).

A worthwhile detour here is made by turning right along Hoang Van Thu, then left into Hoang Dieu. At the corner of Phan Dinh Phung on the right (south-east corner) is another Neo-Classical building with a steep mansard roof and round oriole windows, now occupied by the Military Petrochemical Stock Company. Almost opposite is the Cua Bac Catholic Church, again, designed by Hebrard and completed in 1925. Contrasting with Hebrard's signature two-tier tile roofs of the octagonal cupola over the apse, the vertical tower is vaguely redolent of Italian bell towers.

A few yards further along Phan Dinh Phung is the only remaining structure of the Nguyen Citadel apart from the flag tower, the old north gate (Cua Bac), its high-arched entrance easily high enough to accommodate elephants, if there happened to be any about. Even when it was built, 1812, it was a bit late for elephants, but imperial pomp dies slowly. With its forbidding brick and stone walls, unrelieved by decoration, it bears a resemblance on a smaller scale to Ngo Mon (gate) of the Nguyen dynasty citadel in Hue. Its two-tier tile roofs with turned-up corners relieve the austerity and render it picturesque. A plaque in French dated 25 April 1882, records the bombardment of the citadel by cannons from French gunboats on the Red river, *'surprise et fanfare.'*

Returning along Phan Dinh Phung and turning left into Hung Vuong, at the northwest corner of Ba Dinh is . . .

PRESIDENTIAL PALACE *(Toa Nha Quoc Hoi)*

Built as the *Hôtel de la Résidence Supérieure du Tonkin,* it was designed by Adolphe Bussy and completed in 1919. It could be a French private *hôtel* lifted from the Second Empire with its sloping tile roofs, the two wings in strict symmetry, the windows of the facade bearing protruding medallions, framed by classic Ionic pillars. Entered via a flared central stairway of honour or the curving ramp, the ornate iron gates suggest a hint of *art nouveau* style. These days it is used to receive visiting heads of state and is therefore closed to the public.

Heading south along Hung Vuong, named after the first pre-historic era Hung king, several more embassies are housed in former French villas.

FINE ARTS MUSEUM *(Vien Bao Tang My Thuat)*

At the corner of Cao Ba Quat (66 Nguyen Thai Hoc Street), this three-storey building was formerly the Pugier School for Girls, dating from 1898. The impressive tile-roofed circular entrance canopy is supported by smooth circular pillars, their bases decorated with a lotus motif. The plain stucco facade is broken by stubby pillars between the shuttered windows of the top two floors. Above the shallow, circular tiled roof is a gable with turned-up corners in the style of a pagoda, its overlapping supporting beams echoing those of Hebrard in his museum for *l'Ecole Française d'Extrême Orient,* now the History Museum. Inside, the dark-stained wooden banisters of the stairs, elegantly curled at the base, look to be original.

The ground floor displays several prehistoric bronzes, a few fine Cham statues and gilt religious sculpture from the Ly and Tran dynasties. The collection of ceramics from the eleventh to twentieth century is housed in the basement. The first floor holds lacquer paintings – a fine lacquer screen with cranes and waterfowl in a garden on one side, a procession to a pagoda on the other, dated 1935 – traditional Hong Do and Hang Trong woodblock prints and sculpture from the first half of the twentieth century. Here, the environment of war begins to express itself in the paintings, even in the lacquer.

The second floor is given over to paintings in oil and watercolours on paper and silk. The deep longing for peace and normality represented by a painting depicting a jolly village scene becomes clear when one reads the title and the date, *The Days of my Dream, 1969* – in the midst of the Vietnam War.

Turning (left) into Le Hong Phong Street, the grand villas, now embassies in this street were designed mainly by French-trained Vietnamese architects. Look for the Romanian Embassy at number 5, the Singaporean Embassy at numbers 41 and 43, and the World Wildlife Fund at number 53 Le Hong Phong.

As Ba Dinh Square is Vietnam's official centre of government, naturally this area is very much associated with Ho Chi Minh, who lived nearby.

(See Hanoi's Ho Chi Minh Trail chapter, also the Temple of Literature chapter as both are virtually round the corner.)

HANOI'S HO CHI MINH TRAIL

Affairs of state take precedence over those of the family
– Vietnamese proverb

BA DINH SQUARE

Ho Chi Minh read out his historic, freshly penned Declaration of Independence for the Socialist Republic of Vietnam in Ba Dinh Square on 2 September 1945. It is said that virtually the entire Vietnamese population of Hanoi was in attendance.

According to historian, Nguyen Vinh Phuc, Ho Chi Minh's platform, covered in red cloth, was installed in the middle of the square where half a million people had gathered to hear. Following a salute to the flag and Ho Chi Minh's speech came the swearing-in ceremony of the new Provisional Government. Then the newly appointed Minister of Internal Affairs – Vo Nguyen Giap, later the victorious general of the Vietnam War – discussed the domestic situation and the new government's policies. The Minister of Propaganda, Tran Huy Lieu, then rose to his feet and described the handing over of the imperial symbols of power by representatives of the Nguyen dynasty to representatives of the new Communist Government. The royal seal and the sword were shown to the people and the gathering ended with the jubilant crowd marching through the streets of Hanoi.

Twenty-four years later, Ho Chi Minh died on Vietnam's national holiday, 2 September 1969. Seven days later on 9 September 1969, his death was announced – his death having gone unannounced on the day of his death to avoid marring the national holiday. A solemn memorial service in his honour was held in Ba Dinh Square. A hundred thousand people from all over the country and thirty-four international delegations attended. Today, a flagpole stands in the centre of this vast sea of evergreen grass (320 x 100metres). Ba Dinh is composed of one hundred sixty-eight small squares of grass to represent the rice paddies of Vietnam and it is here that National Day celebrations with military parades take place. Ba Dinh has become a sacred place to patriotic Hanoians.

HO CHI MINH'S MAUSOLEUM *(Chu Tich Ho Chi Minh)*

At the centre of the west side of Ba Dinh Square looms the grey granite and marble bulk of Ho Chi Minh's Mausoleum. Despite his request that his ashes be scattered throughout his beloved homeland, in a modern version of ancestor veneration, when he died Ho Chi Minh's body was embalmed and put on display in a modern temple where people could come to pay their respects.

After queuing, just inside the marble foyer, the visitor is greeted with his words: 'Nothing is more important than independence and freedom.' His slight, pale body lies under glass upstairs, dimly lit, his thin hands resting on the black silk coffin covers. Nothing of his reputedly magnetic, charismatic personality remains, but this slim, lifeless form of a man continues to inspire the crowds of visitors who come from afar and the queues of school children who file past his coffin when he is in residence (closed October and November).

Virtually beside Ho Chi Minh's Mausoleum is . . .

THE ONE PILLAR PAGODA *(Chua Mot Cot)*

Nothing to do with Ho Chi Minh, but as it is nearby, this small, charming pagoda is one of the earliest historic structures of the Ly dynasty. It is not the original built by Emperor Ly Thai Tong in 1049. The original was blown up in a vengeful act by the departing French in 1954. But apart from the base, Hanoians rebuilt an exact replica of the original.

This being Vietnam, of course, there is a story. It seems that Emperor Ly Thai Tong had not produced an heir. He prayed to the goddess Quan Am and subsequently had a dream in which the goddess, sitting on her lotus throne, handed him a baby.

A bit later, the happy emperor was blessed with a fine, healthy son, born of a common village girl he had taken as wife. In gratitude, he built the pagoda to honour the goddess Quan Am. This tiny wooden structure of only three square metres holds a statue of Quan Am. It is indeed supported by a single column (these days concrete), rising from an artificial pond, the entire structure intended to represent a lotus blossom, the Buddhist symbol of purity. Opposite the One Pillar Pagoda is . . .

PAGODA OF THE LASTING BLESSING *(Dien Huin)*

The hall of this Buddhist pagoda has wide, open doors to the right of the courtyard. Fortuitously, I am accompanied by my Buddhist friend, who explains why an extended family has spread a meal out on mats: 'performing the rituals following a death.' When someone dies, the family awaits the judgments in heaven, then seven days after the death, goes to a pagoda to pay respects and to pray for blessings for the dead person to mitigate the judgments. One begins to understand why an extended family and leaving offspring are important.

The pagoda holds three statues wearing flat hats rather like mortarboards – 'Brahmanism, they govern heaven, but today are transformed into kings, one responsible for births, the other for deaths,' my friend explains. Behind the three kings is a busily carved openwork, gilt nine-dragon altar to Sakyamuni as a baby.

'The nine dragons supplied water at his birth, after which he took seven steps, declaring, "There is only one Buddha – Buddha is everywhere around us, in heaven and in human beings."'

The temple to the left of the courtyard holding a large statue of a monk, is dedicated to 'resident monk patriots and the cult of the holy mothers,' who joined the assemblage of religious personages occupying Vietnamese temples. The only religion that refused to integrate has been Catholicism.

Neither of these pagodas, of course, has anything to do with Ho Chi Minh.

HO CHI MINH'S HOUSE AND GARDEN *(Nh San Bac Ho)*

Not far from his mausoleum is Uncle Ho's stilt house. Following independence from the French in 1954, the new president, unwilling to occupy the pretentious President's Palace, had an unassuming wooden house built for himself behind the palace, modelling it in the style of a stilt house built by an ethnic minority. A wooden house with open sides hung with split bamboo screens, the ground floor he used for meetings. Here are the old-fashioned telephone and the table around which he sat with his Politboro. Upstairs are his bedroom and study, sparsely furnished with bed and desks and an old-fashioned radio. After all, this was a man who had lived in the jungle near the Chinese border for some time; he was accustomed to a Spartan lifestyle. It is said that Ho Chi Minh lived here for the last eleven years of his life, even part of the time during the Vietnam War – there was an underground bunker nearby. Walking around his home and through his garden, gazing at his fish pond, one feels the humanness of the man.

HO CHI MINH MUSEUM *(Bao Tang Ho Chi Minh)*

Quite near Ho Chi Minh's stilt house is the museum dedicated to his memory. From a central dais, the colossal statue of the father of his country raises a hand in greeting to the crowds in the foyer of this slightly baffling edifice of floating stairs and marble platforms. Children of ten or eleven approach with, 'Hello, how are you?' before skittering away again. Disregarding kings and queens, Britain seems to lack an equivalent beloved paternal figure. Churchill? Not quite. The scene brings back memories of my visits to the Washington and Lincoln Memorials and to Jefferson's home at Monticello.

I follow the crowd past a reconstruction of Uncle Ho's humble thatched childhood home and peer at his school records. Poor chap, he came number two in his class and I feel sorry for him, having to suffer this ignominious lack of academic privacy in a country where scholarly achievement is so highly esteemed.

Upstairs, a hand-written sign reads 'Concert' with an arrow. Pushing through the swinging doors, I catch the sound of plucked strings and following my ears, come to a small room where a few chairs have been set out. Four young women, each wearing a different ethnic costume, motion to sit down.

To my delight there is an instrument I haven't seen before, a row of huge horizontal bamboo pipes, which the musician 'plays' by clapping her cupped hands at the end of each pipe. Called *c'long put,* it makes a breathy tone somewhat similar to Peruvian pipes and comes from one of the ethnic hill tribes. Between numbers, one of the musicians hands out tiny cups of green tea. To end of their performance, to my bemused surprise they play *Auld Lang Syne,* handing one member of the audience a red rose and in jest, plop a straw peasant hat on my head. For the privilege of listening, we are invited to buy a CD or a tape of their music, or there is a wooden box on the table for donations.

THE TEMPLE OF LITERATURE

A man without education is an uncut gem
– Vietnamese proverb

Imagine a church dedicated to Saint Shakespeare. For all of the deep respect and affection that we hold for our beloved poet and playwright, we do not quite worship him. But in Vietnam, as scholarship ranks next to godliness, they have built a Confucian Temple of Literature.

Just south of where the south gate of the old Citadel opened, (south of the Museum of Fine Arts), stands one of Hanoi's oldest and most significant temples and educational establishments. A few years ago, a young student named Ngoc, who was studying languages and international affairs, first led me through the Temple of Literature. As we arrived, several girls in pink *ao dais,* the national costume (pronounced ow as in now, zai) – long side-slit tunics over flowing trousers – were coming out, having posed for wedding photographs.

At the three-arched stone entrance gate, Ngoc pointed out two seemingly inconsequential stelae, 'Commanding all who would enter to dismount (from their palanquins) and show respect – including the emperor,' Ngoc announced. This was my first indication that scholarship had for so long been held in such high esteem in Vietnam.

'In higher esteem even than royalty,' Ngoc assured me, her eyes wide.

While Britain was still wallowing in the dark ages – two centuries before the founding of Oxford, one century before Bologna – Vietnam was busy establishing a university. Van Mieu, literally the Temple of Literature, first opened its doors in 1070 as 'an altar to Confucius' under Emperor Ly Thanh Tong. Six years later, it became 'the Royal College for the Teaching of Royal Princes to Rule.'

Considering that an emperor might have more than a hundred wives or concubines, naturally there would have been quite a few young princes to educate. Only one year later, Van Mieu began to admit the sons of mandarins and from that time on, it became known as the College for the Sons of the Nation (Van Mieu-Quoc Tu Giam).

Somewhat later, the College expanded further, this time admitting those who had succeeded in passing regional examinations, thus creating very early in the country's history, a meritocracy of social mobility through education, at least for those whose families who were wealthy enough to allow a son to immerse himself in books for several years as a financially unproductive member of the family.

At the Great Portico, a two-storey gate under a two-tiered tile roof, Ngoc began my tutelage on the subject of dragons. Pointing to the image of a flying dragon, 'Symbol of good luck, royalty, and later, of the mandarinate. Eventually, the dragon also came to signify the rank of the doctoral degree *(tien si)*. The image of the descending tiger, coming down from the mountain to help humanity, serves as a symbol of strength and power. The tiger came to signify the rank of the bachelor degree *(cu nhan).'*

She recited the translation of the inscription in Chinese characters over the main entrance: 'Among the doctrines of the world, ours is the best and is revered by all culture-starved lands.' No wonder there was a head-on clash with the French!

Another modest inscription reads: 'Of all the temples devoted to literature, this is the head; the perfume of culture floats throughout the millennia.' Hanoi's Temple of Literature was considered to be the veritable fountain of Vietnamese erudition.

Although no longer a university, the Temple of Literature remains an oasis of quietude in the bustle and cacophony of Hanoi's busy street life. A central path, symbolic of the Confucian Middle Way or Golden Mean, divides the walled temple complex of five successive courtyards.

No doubt the grandiose names of the gates and the inscriptions throughout were meant to inspire the neophyte scholars towards high intellectual attainment, rather like the portraits of illustrious alumnae that throng the halls of Western universities. Old frangipani and banyan trees spread their shade over the first two grassy courtyards where a few students still

111

sprawled over their books, although the Temple of Literature ceased to be an active educational establishment a century ago. This must be one of the few quiet and most inspiring places in Hanoi to study. Bright pink lotus blossoms float amongst a carpet of green leaf pads in the rectangular lily ponds to left and right of the central path, exactly symmetrical and perfectly balanced as everything must be in a Confucian environment.

Two carp perch nose down on the roof ridges of the gate leading to the second courtyard: 'Paying obeisance to a flask of nectar from heaven,' explained Ngoc, doubtless, the nectar of Confucianism.

'The carp symbolize students on their way to becoming mandarins. Legend has it that the carp that succeed in passing through a natural stone arch known as the Gate of Emperor Vu in the Hoang Ho river during the violent tides of the third lunar month, become dragons. Successful mandarin examination candidates are likened to the carp that have passed through the arch.' In another version, fish aspiring to dragon-hood have to swim up three waterfalls, a process that takes a thousand years. In this version, the carp represent a symbol of the common people, swimming up from the grass roots of a pond by way of three levels of examinations (local, provincial and royal) to the status of mandarins.

Smaller gateways at the far extremities of this wall bear more inscriptions in *chu nom* Chinese ideograms: Accomplished Virtue on the right, Attained Talent on the left. As every student had to be able to read *chu nom* ideograms to be admitted to the college, these inscriptions would have admonished them daily. Nowadays, only a few scholars devote themselves to the old *chu nom* texts, tenuously preserving a link with the country's rich traditional literature and culture.

Now, visiting again, by nine o'clock in the morning the cicadas are already sawing away in heated competition with the frogs. On the far side of the second courtyard stands the rather glorious two-storey, red lacquered Constellation of Literature Pavilion (Khue Van Cac).

'This pavilion was considered to be rich in the complementary symbolism of *yin* and *yang*, the union of contrasting parts, according to the cosmic Great Primary Principle.' The pavilion is also extremely orientally picturesque.

The pavilion bears the inscriptions: 'Just as the Khue constellation shines in the sky, the humanities shine everywhere' – a sentiment to warm the hearts of Western humanities academics, who might sometimes feel under-rated. The opposite, parallel sentence reads: 'The deep waters of the royal college perpetuate the fountain of the doctrine.' Quite so.

Two smaller gates lead from this courtyard. The one on the right, named the Crystallization of Letters, refers to 'literary expression that is profound and full of feeling.' The one on the left, the Magnificence of Letters, 'pays homage to ideas that are well and beautifully expressed.' Like many a hopeful student before me, I make sure I pass through both gates, hoping the pretentious sentiments will have some osmotic effect.

In the Garden of the Stelae, the square pond known as the Well of Heavenly Clarity has lost its clarity. Despite the heat, I am not the least bit tempted to leap into its frothy opaque greenery. Two lines of stone stelae, each stele solidly planted on the back of a stone turtle, the symbol of longevity, list the names, native villages and ages of the successful doctoral candidates from 1442 to 1779. The earliest turtles hold their stone heads high. The later, less snooty turtles merely poke their heads out of their shells, resting their weighty chins.

The oldest stele dated 1442, carved by order of Emperor Le Thai Tong, bears a noble inscription: 'So the erection of this stele will be of great help, a warning to the wicked and an encouragement to honest persons: knowing the past and looking to the future helps to foster the dignity of scholars and to consolidate the state.' A sentiment that could happily apply today – or for any age.

Having been born in a country that rarely attracts the erudite or even the wise to political leadership, I especially appreciate the following: 'Virtuous and talented men are the life-breath of the nation.'

The message on the stele of 1592 expresses a rather wistful hope: 'Heaven has ushered in an era of renewal. The world has opened a period of cultural restoration.'

Ngoc had explained that Van Mieu represented far more than just an educational establishment of learning for learning's sake, however much learning was lauded. Those who passed its bachelor and doctoral degrees were awarded posts as mandarins

113

commensurate with their academic achievements. For centuries it was literally the college for training the nation's administrators, its civil servants and rulers. Had Ngoc been born even a century earlier – as a boy – she would have studied here. For candidates who passed all four examinations, the final question was set by the emperor himself and it was he who decided the order of merit for the doctoral candidates at the top of each class.

Students of all ages studied together. A decree of 1185 set the lower age limit at fifteen; there was no upper limit. The length of study varied. Examinations were usually held every three years, sometimes as infrequently as seven.

The multi-stage examination process lasted several months. The first was to pass a regional examination held triennially. Successful candidates then walked to Hanoi from wherever they lived in the country, carrying their sleeping mats, brushes and ink stones in order to sit the four-part Thi Hoi examination.

It is thought that the examinations in Hanoi were held near the National Library as suggested by the street name, Examination Street (Trang Thi). With maybe four hundred fifty to six thousand candidates sitting, the examination area would have needed to be extensive. I wonder if they erected thatched roofs to protect the poor examinees from the sun and rain? If the culmination of the examinations was in the third lunar month – usually, torridly hot April, the capital would have been quite chilly and drizzly at the beginning of the exams and hot and steamy by the time they ended.

At the first doctoral examination, only three candidates passed; at the second, seven; at the third, the success rate rose to twenty-three.

Part I of the examinations posed questions from the five Confucian classics: *The Great Study, The Golden Mean, The Analects* (Conversations between Confucius and His Disciples) and *The Works of Mencius (The Upper Book* and *The Lower Book)*. Plus the five additional works: *The Odes, The Annals, The Book of Change, Rites and Ceremonies* and *The Spring and Autumn Annals.*

In Part II, the candidate had to write as though he were the emperor, discussing matters of state.

In Part III, the candidate was asked to compose two different genres of poems on given topics. The *tho phu* was a poem of twenty-eight characters, four lines of seven characters. The *phu* was a prose poem of eight, seven-character lines.

In Part IV, the candidate was asked to comment on how to handle problems facing the country, drawing from his knowledge of Confucian classics and the history of previous dynasties.

After that first visit to the Temple of Literature, it began to dawn on me just how deeply embedded in the Vietnamese psyche the thirst for learning and poetry are. If every civil servant had to prove himself a poet for nearly a thousand years, it is hardly any wonder that even today, every Vietnamese considers himself or herself to be a poet. And it comes as no surprise then, that many of the most brilliant statesmen were also fine poets.

One example was Nguyen Trai, the moving spirit and strategist behind the victorious fifteenth century battle against the Chinese led by General Le Loi, he of the magic sword. Nguyen Trai is still honoured as one of Vietnam's greatest statesmen and in addition to his involvement in matters of state, he also found time to serve as a Royal Examiner.

The Call of the Roll, the publication of successful candidates on the third day of the third lunar month, was a glorious event for the literati. To indicate success, the emperor handed each successful doctoral candidate a poinsettia blossom, here known as 'the doctoral flower'. Upon successful doctoral candidates he bestowed favour, mandarin ranks, mandarin bonnets and robes.

He feted them with a banquet in Quynh Lam palace and when they returned to their native villages, they travelled in state on horseback with footmen carrying fringed parasols to protect them from the sun, and footmen bearing banners to herald the new doctors' approach, as can be seen in many paintings and tableaux in mosaic and lacquer. Only 2,313 candidates were awarded the title of doctor between 1070 and 1779, most in their twenties and thirties. The youngest ever was eighteen, the eldest sixty-one.

Another tile-roofed structure, the Gate of the Great Synthesis, some call it the Gate of Great Success, leads to a fourth courtyard, the Courtyard of the Sages. I was delighted that Ngoc knew the meanings of the old *cho nom* characters.

'The side gates laud the beauty and value of Confucian doctrine as its influence echoes throughout the world. The Gate of the Golden Sound evokes the first peel of the bell; the Gate of Jade Resonance reflects the last reverberation of a gong.'

Classes were held in two buildings alongside the Courtyard of the Sages (now souvenir shops). In the grounds beyond, there had been dormitories (destroyed by bombs). There had even been a print shop for school texts.

In the Courtyard of Sages, where chess games using human chess pieces still take place during the Vietnamese lunar New Year *(Tet)* celebrations, an incense jar, perhaps representing Confucian nectar, is guarded by two leafy topiary cranes, their bodies abloom with tiny white flowers.

On the steps of the Great House of Ceremonies, where the emperor once passed to make his offering at the altar of Confucius and the new doctoral laureates would have entered to express their gratitude, two girls wearing *ao dais* pose for photographs. Inside, golden dragons flick their tails amongst clouds on the thick red lacquered columns of the temple.

Two lanky bronze cranes, the birds of transport between heaven and earth, stand balanced on the backs of bronze turtles on each side of the altar, eternally awaiting take-off. A lacquered, carved 'tapestry' drapes itself above the altar and the scent of burning joss sticks rises in a wisp of smoke towards the rafters as a couple of contemporary students light offerings to invoke the spirit of Confucius to help them through upcoming exams.

Inscribed over the altar are the words: 'Teacher of thousands of generations.' The tinkling sound of traditional Vietnamese music drifts from the Sanctuary building just behind the House of Ceremonies, its rooftop ridge lines ablaze with jubilant dragons making obeisance to the moon – the carp have succeeded in becoming dragons. In the central place of honour in the House of Ceremonies, a jolly red giant statue of Confucius sits between four disciples, two on each side, naturally. The bright red lacquered statue of Confucius looks quite pleased and happy, the palms of his hands not quite touching as though he were clapping. A tableau honours the fourteenth century scholar, Chu Van An (1292-1370), rector of the national university for forty years, whose name has come to be revered as an embodiment of integrity and devotion to scholarship.

'The father of education in Vietnam,' Ngoc had said reverently. One of his short poems demonstrates the subtlety of expression in those distant times and from the far side of the world, hints of a pre-Wordsworthian sentiment:

Spring Morning

In the hut in the mountains one is free the live long day
A clump of bamboo leaning o'er screens from cold mountain air
Green grows the grass and the sky reels in joy
Late lingers the dew in the cups of scarlet flowers
The man alone with the lonely cloud clings to the mountain side
His spirit like water in old wells lies still, unshaken by any tremor
As the sweet pine logs sink to ash the pot for tea stops boiling
A murmur of birds from the deeps of the ravine bring him back
    from the light sleep of Spring.
(tr Huu Ngoc)

Westerners might refute whether classical literature provides a proper preparation for governing a nation, but the system of Confucian ethics based on central control served both China and Vietnam for many centuries as a framework for the society of the day – and the tradition of central control remains today.

Ironically, it was the Confucian Nguyen dynasty that ended Van Mieu's function as the nation's first university. Having moved the capital to Hue with their ascent to power in the nineteenth century, they also 'moved' the Temple of Literature, or more realistically, built one of their own.

The last examinations at Hanoi's Temple of Literature took place in 1919.

TOWARDS WESTLAKE AND BEYOND

New spirits for old ones
– Vietnamese proverb

Approaching West Lake, just before the dyke on the right stands Quan Than temple, one of Hanoi's oldest. First built in 1010 by Emperor Ly Thai To, the founder of Thang Long, it was rebuilt in 1677. The present, very fine building dates from 1893; it was last restored in 1998.

The word Quan indicates that this is a Taoist temple. It honours Tran Vu, guardian of the north in Taoism. Tran Vu was also a legendary figure who aided the pre-historic Hung King, An Duong Vuong, in defeating the devils who threatened the building of his citadel at Co Loa – the pre-historic Viet capital twelve miles (20 km) north of Hanoi. Considered the protector of the country in times of adversity, Than Vu has inspired generations of heroes. The Vietnamese preserve their sense of cultural identity and keep their long history of struggle, survival and victory very much alive by commemorating these ancient, even pre-historic heroes in their temples.

At nine in the morning, three young men and a girl wearing red sashes and loose trousers are doing energetic *kung fu* exercises in the courtyard in front of the red lacquer and gilt temple doors. Kneeling carp and spiky dragons dance along the roof ridge, admiring a round disc, the moon. Inside, worshippers are moving about, lighting joss sticks, kneeling, raising and lowering their hands in devotion before the altars.

Quan Than temple is famous for the colossal black bronze figure of Tran Vu, cast in 1667 – the figure of a man, his left hand in a *mudra* position, his right hand holding a sword around which a snake is entwined, a turtle between his feet. The majestic bronze sits high above the uppermost altar, looking down over the giant cranes and the weapons of power attached to long pikes. People pass, touching his toes in an act of homage. Measuring more than four meters high (13 ft), this immense statue weighs

118

nearly four tons and is considered by many to be a masterpiece of Hanoi bronze casting. The small stone statue (to the right), sculpted to honour the creator by his admiring disciples, is thought to represent Trum Trong, who cast the colossal bronze.

In feudal times the banks of West Lake, then known as the Lake of Mists, were lined by royal villas and those of courtiers and generals, alas, destroyed as dynasties came and went. Until fairly recently, the banks of West Lake (Ho Tay), Hanoi's largest lake, roughly eight miles (13 km) in periphery, held a collection of flower producing villages. Come the early nineties, this was where the newly rich built their toy town houses. Bursting out of their past austerity, exuberantly displaying every architectural fantasy imaginable, terraces and balconies bulging with curling wrought-iron and classical balustrades, this wildly eclectic style has now become so common throughout Hanoi that they have lost their novelty. Since then, new satellite suburbs have begun to spring up in the suburbs of Hanoi.

Leaving Quan Than temple, approaching West Lake is a dyke called Youth Road (Duong Thong Nien), built by villagers in the seventeenth century. Lined with frangipani trees, the dyke separates the smaller White Silk Lake (Ho Truc Bach) on the right from West Lake (Ho Tay).

Naturally, there are stories and legends in regard to both lakes. The mushroom-shaped peninsula that extends into White Silk Lake has been a prime piece of residential property for a long time. Here, an eighteenth century Trinh lord built a summer palace, where it is said that disagreeable concubines were locked away and forced to weave endless white silk for the Trinh princesses, hence, the name of the lake.

Two legends surround the origin of West Lake itself. In one, an eleventh century monk who had rendered services to the emperor of China, was allowed to bring back a large quantity of bronze to cast a bell. When the huge bell tolled, the sound carried as far as China and the golden calf, mistaking it for the call of his buffalo mother, rushed south to find her. In his headlong charge, the giant calf turned up great mounds of earth. When the bell stopped tolling, the calf stopped, confused, turning this way and that, creating a deep hollow that filled with water, West Lake. The other legend relates to a nine-tailed fox, slain by the dragon king, Lan Long Quan of the pre-historic Lac people, the shadowy

119

ancestors of the Viets. The fox had been molesting maidens, so the dragon king flooded the evil fox's lair, creating West Lake. Dragons go right back to the creation myth of the Viet people – the legend that the pre-historic Hung kings were descendants of the dragon of the seas and the fairy of the mountains.

The geographical explanation for the lakes is that both West Lake (Ho Tay) and White Silk Lake(Ho Truc Bach), earlier a part of Ho Tay, lay in the former riverbed of the Red river (Song Hong). When the river changed its course to the east, the shallow lake was left.

Along the dyke where the road bends slightly, stands a small memorial on the right, dedicated to teams of anti-aircraft gunners stationed here during the Vietnam War. But instead of the gunners, rather unexpectedly, the memorial represents an American pilot who dropped from the sky – the downing of Navy Lt Cdr John McCain, who parachuted into White Silk Lake, 10 October 1967. He resided for more than five years as a guest of the Hanoi Hilton prison. Years later, he became a US senator and in 2008, the Republican candidate for the US presidency.

Past the swan boats and a floating restaurant on the left about halfway across the dyke dividing the two lakes, is the oldest pagoda, not only in Hanoi but in all of Vietnam, Tran Quoc.

In 544, Ly Bi led an insurrection and defeated the Liang (Chinese), providing a brief respite from Chinese rule. He proclaimed himself emperor, established the Van Xuan kingdom and built a fortress on the To Lich river. To commemorate his victory, he built the Nation Founding Pagoda (Khai Quoc) beside the Red river. In 580 an imminent Indian monk came to this pagoda and preached. After a landslide, the pagoda was moved to West Lake in 1680 where it is now known as Tran Quoc.

Here, it originally stood on an island until the local Yen Phu villagers built the dyke, creating the two lakes and a causeway to reach the pagoda. Slender-trunked areca palms line the causeway, these days crowded with tightly parked motorbikes.

Entrance is past the brick stupas holding the remains of former monks of this pagoda and an eleven-tier bell tower. Normally, stupas are placed at the back of a pagoda, but the original entrance to this pagoda was by boat on the opposite side, facing the lake. The temple on the right is dedicated to the mother goddesses and former patriarch monks of this pagoda.

As in temples throughout Vietnam, the holy mothers can be identified by the colour of their gowns: red for the skies, green for mountains and forests, white for the waters. The Indian monk, Bodhidharma (470-543), who preached here and founded the Zen sect in China, (the Thien sect in Vietnam), occupies the place of honour (same chap we met earlier at Vu Thach pagoda near Hoan Kiem lake). Another statue of him stands outside between the monks' quarters and the sanctuary. Legend has it that after his death he was seen with one sandal at the end of a stick over his shoulder, crossing a river en route to his homeland. It is also said that upon unearthing his grave (according to custom, to rebury his bones after one year) that there was, indeed, only one sandal! It's a long walk to India, even for an immortal.

Throughout the centuries, the pagoda has had numerous restorations, necessitated by a hot and cold, damp climate. One of its distinguishing characteristics, architecturally, is its inclining H-shape, the connecting bar the rectangular space holding successively higher altars.

Crowds of Vietnamese are bringing offerings, plates of fruit and vases of flowers, and leaving *dong* notes on the several altars. The exquisite, intricately carved gilt work framing the beams and pillars is worthy of a museum, but happily, remains in daily use.

The first altar holds a red robed statue, no less a personage than the guardian of the pagoda, flanked to one side by a warrior-soldier under a helmet and a civilian mandarin in a winged hat on the other. He is no doubt aided by two huge, tubby *dvarapala* wearing armour. The guardian with the pink face holds the pearl of wisdom; the one with the red face, a stick in his hand, punishes evil. They are both guardians of the law and because they usually appear as larger-than-life statues, the Vietnamese will liken anyone of particularly large stature to a *dvarapala*.

There is also an altar to Quan Cong, the same third century Chinese general honoured in Ngoc Son Temple in Hoan Kiem, attended by Quan Binh, his son, and Chau Xuong, a military comrade. One sometimes feels that the Vietnamese abhorrence of privacy extends to their deities – no one should be left alone.

Here the roll-call of deities is a bit overwhelming. The hall of worship holds a fine, nine-dragon altar to Sakyamuni, the baby Buddha, who was bathed at birth by the dragons after which he took seven steps. His right hand is pointing to the sky, his left to

121

the earth, signifying that he is the mediator between heaven and earth. Higher up sits a magnificent gilt Quan Yin, goddess of the many arms, she of a thousand eyes and ears and in the uppermost position, the three golden Buddhas of the past, present and future, sitting side by side. Three more Buddhas are repeated at ever-rising heights through the centre of the hall, sitting on lotuses, the symbol of purity – as it blooms unaffected by the muddy earth from which it grows.

Amitaba, Buddha of the present, who rules over the pure land of all bliss, occupies the next tier. Beside him stand two *bodhisattvas:* Mahasthamprapra, who holds the book of trusts and Avalokiteshvara, who holds a bottle of nectar. Sakyamuni, Buddha of the present, who lived in India in the sixth century BC, occupies the next level, flanked by his disciples: his cousin and favourite, Ananda, and his senior disciple, Kasyapa.

At the top level sits the fat and happy Maitreya, Buddha of the future, accompanied at each side by *bodhisattvas:* Manjusri, symbolic of wisdom and intelligence and Samantabhadra, embodying the law of Buddhist teaching.

Rarely in North Vietnam, this pagoda holds a gilt reclining Buddha, more commonly found in the Hinayana (Lesser Vehicle) Buddhist pagodas of Laos, Thailand and Cambodia.

The kings of hell, wearing mortarboards, five each side, line the aisles. Hell to the Vietnamese, or one should say in Buddhism, does not represent eternal damnation – there are ten hells to fit each sin or crime and once the sinner has been punished, he moves on to the next until he has finished his punishments. Then he is reborn, depending upon his virtue or otherwise as a king or mandarin, if he has been especially good; at the second level as a rich man or a noble; at the third as a widow, spinster, bachelor or poor person. Really immoral behaviour means that he will be reborn, again in descending order, as a bird, an animal, an insect, a crab or a fish. I am a bit surprised that fish and crabs don't outrank mosquitoes and flies.

An altar at the rear of the hall is dedicated to the saint of kindness, Ananda, Buddha's cousin and favourite disciple, wearing a tall hexagonal crown. There is some dispute about another altar in which the figure robed in red, wearing a black crown under a gold-edged drape. Some say it is an altar to the Tran dynasty, the golden age of Buddhism in Vietnam.

Others say that it is General Tran Hung Dao (without the armour), who defeated the Mongols. The pagoda contains fourteen stelae from the fourteenth and fifteenth centuries, used in centuries past to teach monks of the Vo Ngon Thong sect. Numerous monks from this sect served as counsellors to succeeding emperors in the imperial court. So not only is this the oldest pagoda in the nation, it also produced advisers who influenced the nation's rulers down the centuries.

Moving on across the dyke past floating restaurants, the Intercontinental Hotel looms on the right. When I first came to Hanoi in 1997, there were only two hotels of any note at West Lake, the Cuban-built Thang Loi on the east bank and the Regency in the south-west. What started to be a Sheraton – building stopped abruptly in the nineties during the South-East Asian financial crisis – first metamorphosed into the five-star Sofitel Plaza and later, into the Intercontinental, opened in 2007.

Bending sharply left, skirting the east bank of Ho Tay, a jumble of high-rise mini-towers of the newly affluent crowd the narrow road. Nearly all of the fields of flowers that used to line the lake shore have disappeared under new buildings. Down a narrow lane, Yen Phu pagoda, named after this old village that built the dykes, makes a pleasant stop. No crowds here, a few elderly women fuss about, arranging flowers and offerings.

The official name of the pagoda is Khanh Hung. Here, stone peacocks strut across the tiled roof. A portrait of Ho Chi Minh stares from the lowest altar, behind which stands a lacquered royal funeral palanquin. Oddly, in the place of honour, four pale, chubby statues wearing turbans and colourful tunics, kneel at a low table. A sign reads 'Quan Chu', but who are they? I find no one who can tell me!

The temple to the left holds another funerary palanquin and figures of the three holy mothers in glass cases. This pagoda has a touching story. It is said that the pagoda was first built at the beginning of the Christian era – it holds an imperial edict dated 1640 – and a further twenty-three imperial edicts, which relate to the following legend. Under the domination of the Han Chinese, a woman called Phuong Dung came often to this pagoda to meditate. She had two sons. Around the year 40 AD, the two Trung sisters rose up with the people in revolt against the invaders, chasing them out of the country. Phuong Dung and her two sons had participated in this war against the Han enemies. The villagers therefore built the temple dedicated to the cult of this lady and her two sons and an imperial edict bestowed upon them the rank of Protecting Spirits.

Past the Cuban-built Thang Loi Hotel, Nghi Tam village on a tiny peninsula, used to be a flower-growing village.

Quite how we arrived at Kim Lien pagoda is a mystery involving dirt lanes – I was on the back of a *xe om*. Doubtless, a taxi would have found a smoother, perhaps longer route.

Kim Lien pagoda was built on the site of the Tu Hoa palace in the village of Ho Tay (West Lake) and of course, there is a story. It seems that a seventeenth century scholar, Phung Khac Khoan (1528-1613) was out boating one day with friends on Ho Tay when they met a beautiful young woman. They talked and composed poetry together, but when Phung asked her name, she merely smiled, recited a poem, then suddenly vanished. On analysing the poem, Phung realized that she was none other than Lieu Hanh, the holy mother. Following this event, Ho Tay villagers built the Tu Hoa palace and dedicated it to her.

Roughly two centuries later, according to a stele of 1868, in 1771 the Trinh lord ordered Bao Lam pagoda to be moved here from the west bank of Hoan Kiem Lake. He renamed it Kim Lien. Restoration in 1792 gave it its current general appearance of beautiful tiled roofs with curved, turned-up corners. Carved square stone pillars support what now look like freshly tiled roofs. This may be one of Hanoi's oldest, most beautiful and revered pagodas, but as the Vietnamese maintain the fabric of their religious buildings by renewing and restoring as the climate demands, their appearance belies their age.

Here, the intricately carved gilt work over each of the beamed areas are works of art. Two gorgeously gaudy, giant *dharma* statues guard the central sanctuary. The nine-dragon altar is particularly fine, flanked by ranks of kings of hell wearing mortarboards, watched over by a gilt, multi-armed statue with crossed swords above her head, a Quan Am in Tantric form. Still higher sits a placid Buddha, gazed down upon from on high by the three Buddhas of the past, present and future. One of the statues that has puzzled visitors through the years is that of a middle-aged man with a tufted beard, holding a piece of paper and wearing a mandarin hat. Is it one of the Trinh lords or a Buddhist monk who served this pagoda under the Trinhs? No one knows, but it has been established that the statue is more than two hundred years old. Known or unknown, he has collected several plates of fruit offerings and piles of *dong* notes. Beside him is a graceful statue of Vietnam's god of mercy, Quan Am Thi Kinh.

Two lacquered parallel sentences engraved with Han characters translate as: 'widespread morality' *(huang uan)* and 'scene of the happy life in the land of the Buddha' *(lien hoa hai hoi)*, the latter somewhat wistful as the boards are dated 1930 – while the Vietnamese were under French rule.

In a quiet building on the right – temple or pagoda, there are aspects of both – where traditional music tinkles in the background, the baby Sakyamuni is a pudgy toddler wearing only a wide yellow sash. Beside him is Quan Am Thi Kinh and below, fat and happy Maitreya, Buddha of the future. The second altar is dedicated to ancestor monks, five bald-headed, life-sized figures with possibly two late comers, one in each of the side niches.

Continuing along the lake shore, a good many smart, up-market European and Vietnamese restaurants have sprung up here to satisfy the discerning taste of the new residents, Vietnamese as well as foreign. Rounding the northern tip of West Lake, the Regency Hotel and numerous restaurants line the bank.

Shooting off south along Duong Buoi Street beside Thu Le Park, which contains a zoo and an amusement park for children (just behind the Daewoo Hotel, coming from town), the proper entrance to Voi Phuc temple, Hanoi's guardian of the south, is from Kim Ma Street. Two huge stone elephants beside the traditional gate have given the temple its nickname, Kneeling Elephants. A brick path alongside the lake leads to the temple, its founding based on one of my favourite stories.

One historian states that the temple was built in the reign of Ly Thai Tong (1028-1054) and dedicated to Linh Lang, Prince Hoang Chan, Ly Thai Tong's son. According to one story, the prince took part in battles against the Song (Chinese) invaders along the Cau river and fell there.

However, a document still held within the temple tells a more intriguing story – that one of King Ly's concubines, Cao Nuong,

125

went to bathe in the lake and became entangled with a dragon, after which she fell pregnant. When the baby prince was born, twenty-eight dragon scales and seven lines of dots shining like pearls lined his chest! As a young man, he volunteered to command the army and subsequently defeated the Song invaders. The emperor wished to pass on the throne to him, but he refused and asked his father to allow him to live in the place where the temple now stands. One day he was transformed into a black dragon, which wrapped itself around a stone slab and disappeared into the lake. The emperor ordered that a temple be built and dedicated to the prince. Inside are two bronze statues and a huge, mysterious rock with a dipped, concave surface.

SATELLITE CIIES

In the past few years, in a strident attempt to solve the need for accommodation of Hanoi's increasing population and pulsing high density, new satellite suburbs, planned new towns, have popped up west of West Lake and south-west of central Hanoi. To live in one means the peace of wide streets with trees and spacious villas set apart in gardens or a new lifestyle in a sleek, modern high-rise flat, which must seem appealing to families living in cramped quarters, however central.

Ciputra, first of the new planned satellite suburbs, meets the visitor with a grand entrance of white towers. A gated community west of West Lake covering eight hundred sixty-four acres (350 ha) of mixed residential and commercial property, it was financed in the late nineties by an Indonesian group, who had created similar projects in Indonesia. Early on, it attracted the UN International School to build a campus and rumours are flying that the American Embassy may be moving there soon.

Several streets of cream or white, tile-roofed villas with Georgian columns and dark green or brown shutters nestle behind dark green ironwork grills. Some effort has been made to restrain architectural exuberance. However, it breaks free at a junction flourishing a monumental fountain and at another with life-sized galloping bronze horses reminiscent of St Mark's. Ceputra is definitely making a grandiose statement.

The suburb of Linh Dam, south of the city, was financed by a state-owned corporation. Approaching from a narrow road lined by stilt houses, the high-rise orange and green, ten-storey blocks float like a mirage over rice paddies. From a distance it looks so astonishingly Western in aspect that it might be in another country. Once there, the quiet streets are free of traffic. Huge three-storey villas with shuttered windows stand poised behind low walls with gates. Shops, a supermarket, a pharmacy, a doctor and a dentist provide local services.

At another new suburb, My Dinh, in the Tu Lien district to the south-west of Hoan Kiem Lake, the orange, green and yellow apartment blocks shoot up to eighteen storeys and The Manor tower rises in a triangle to twenty-seven storeys. The National Stadium with covered parking, a new National Conference centre and the Institute for Musicology have located here. There's even an impressive New Town Hotel. Nearby, a Korean developer is behind an ambitious seventy-storey, mixed-use tower at the planning stage. When completed in 2010, it will be Vietnam's tallest building.

Friends often ask me if foreigners are allowed to buy property in Vietnam? On 23 May 2008, the Vietnamese Government passed a law allowing certain categories of foreigners to buy flats or apartments beginning in 2009. But they can only buy flats or apartments in developments approved for foreign residency, not houses or land. Ownership is for a term of fifty years, by which time the foreign owners must sell or transfer the property.

Those eligible to buy are limited to foreign firms purchasing housing for staff and four categories of individuals: 1) foreigners working for Vietnamese firms, 2) foreigners married to Vietnamese, 3) foreigners with special skills needed by Vietnam's economy and, 4) foreigners who have been awarded medals or other honours by the Government.

It is not immediately clear how much the new law will differ from the current law allowing foreigners to obtain fifty-year leases on property in Vietnam. Normally in Vietnam, new laws are followed by decrees and circulars clarifying how the law will be implemented. Developers expect that the move from lease to ownership will grant foreigners additional security.

FOOD OF THE PEOPLE

Qualities of the wife are shown by her cooking
– Vietnamese proverb

When I lived in the Old Quarter, my morning walk to Hoan Kiem Lake along Ta Hien Street used to take me past a woman squatting on the pavement, fanning her charcoal brassier, roasting ears of corn or strips of lean pork. The smell of her sizzling pork always made my mouth water, no matter what time of day.

Across the street from my mini-hotel was a tiny, near as damn it, twenty-four-hour noodle soup *(pho)* stall, its boiling cauldron simmering over charcoal in the hollow of a stairwell. Sometimes I would be roused from sleep by the clatter of dishes in the small hours and find the *pho* woman squatting beside a huge aluminium dishpan, washing dishes in the middle of the street or stacking her tiny plastic stools. I always had to check the time to see if she was closing up at four, or opening up again at five. Eventually I learned that she and her daughter ran the *pho* stall in shifts, having come to Hanoi to find an easier way of life than farming on their own.

Around the corner was a similar stall selling *ban cuon,* steamed rolls of rice paper stuffed with fried mushrooms and pork, topped by coriander. Either *pho* or *ban cuon* made a delicious, hearty breakfast, or lunch, or supper.

The Vietnamese tend to think of *pho,* which is practically the national dish, as a specialty of Hanoi, but a bit of research reveals that it probably originated in Nam Dinh Province, about sixty miles (96 km) south-east of Hanoi. Like many other trades in Hanoi, many *pho* cooks tend to come from one village, Van Cu, the only village where people selling *pho* all carry the same family name, Co, which appropriately, translates as great. It is not as one might suppose, a dish that goes back centuries. The first cook to open a *pho* stall in Hanoi was a man named Van, who moved to the city as recently as 1925 and opened a *pho* stall in Hang Hanh Street (off the north-west corner of Hoan Kiem

128

Lake). Several generations of *pho* cooks from Van Cu have moved to Hanoi and the Hanoi Association of Van Cu Residents says that eighty percent of *pho* restaurants in Hanoi are owned by people from their village.

Hanoians wax lyrical over the qualities of *pho* and how much they miss it when they go abroad, although essentially it is beef broth with noodles, slim slivers of beef, onions, herbs and spices. Admittedly, *pho* has a very distinctive, unforgettable flavour. *Pho* cooks guard their secrets as jealously as top chefs, and connoisseurs debate the merits of this *pho* vendor or another. Nearly any Vietnamese restaurant in Hanoi – and throughout the country – has *pho* on the menu, but there are a few rules for finding the best *pho*.

First, it must be in a restaurant or stall that specialists in *pho,* only *pho*. It must have an enormous pot bubbling over charcoal in order to hold lots of bones to give the soup flavour, which more or less eliminates the itinerate vendors who carry small pots and a charcoal burner as well as a table and tiny plastic stools dangling from a bamboo carrying pole – their pots aren't big enough to hold sufficient bones – unless they boiled the bones in the broth at home before setting out.

Choose a stall that offers only beef, the original *pho,* or chicken, but not both. A good *pho* cook steeps the noodles in boiling water to make them hot and soft, then drains them in a basket before transferring the noodles to the *pho* bowl – reheating the noodles for each bowl separately. If the noodles are left to simmer, they go soggy. Each table should have lemon, chilli, chilli sauce, pepper and pickled garlic. Watch out for a shaker that looks like salt – it might be monosodium glutamate. Likewise, if there is sugar or mustard, beware. The *pho* shouldn't need either.

Hanoi food writers – yes, they address themselves to this homely soup – say that the broth should be tasty yet clear, the noodles supple and not crumbly, combined with the right herbs and spices to which, add lemon, chilli and onion. The ingredients of a good *pho* – apart from the beef broth and fresh noodles made from newly harvested rice (much better than dried noodles) – are ginger, cardamom, cinnamon, the mauve leaves of *lang* mint, thin slices of beef and often, spring onions, plus at least five hours of stewing the beef bones. Bean sprouts and large vegetable leaves are not typical of a Hanoi *pho*.

For gourmands, *pho* has been refined into three main types: *pho nuoc*, the traditional dish with noodles, beef, herbs and spices in a big bowl over which the hot broth is poured; *pho xao*, stir-fried *pho* noodles with the meat and herbs – without the broth; and *pho ap chao*, *pho* noodles fried in hot fat until they are brown and crisp, adding the herbs on top at the end.

There are numerous variations on *pho nuoc, pho bo,* which is beef; *pho ga,* which is chicken and *pho lim,* which uses chicken hearts and livers.

In *pho bo chin,* the beef is well boiled, cooled, then cut into very thin slices.

In *pho bo tai,* the fat is removed and cut into thin slices, the meat then placed in a ladle and cooked slightly in a scoop of boiling broth. Then the rare meat is placed on the *pho* noodles in the bowl to which herbs, spices and more hot broth are added – so, *pho bo* – rare!

Pho khong beo means without fat.

In yet another variation, *pho bo tai lan,* the slices of beef are stir-fried until brown.

In *pho tai nam,* cooked beef is combined with raw beef. As you will begin to realize, *pho* is a dish that has become very highly refined.

In a recent take-off, *pho bo sot vang,* no doubt abhorred by purists, the beef is cut into cubes and stewed in wine and spices. So there's a lot more to it than simple beef broth.

A retired *pho* restaurant owner, five of whose nine children now run their own Pho Thin Bo Ho restaurants in Hanoi, declares, 'For a tasty broth, you must use the correct proportion of different kinds of bones, then add salt and fish sauce *(ngoc nam)* at just the right times.'

The Vietnamese eat *pho* with chopsticks in one hand and a spoon in the other. They lift a clutch of noodles with their chopsticks, rest them in the spoon – try it, it isn't easy – and then bite them off, letting the noodles drop back into the bowl. For the Westerner, trained to sit upright at the table, it can be a splashy affair, which explains why even Vietnamese *pho* eaters tend to place their faces rather close to their bowls.

Having mentioned *ngoc mam,* if you have not already encountered it elsewhere in South East Asia or in a Vietnamese restaurant at home, it is a very nutritious, fermented fish sauce, the all-purpose seasoning and substitute for salt in most Vietnamese recipes. The best comes from Phan Thiet on the south coast and from Phu Quoc island off the Mekong Delta in the Gulf of Thailand. Like olive oil, connoisseurs demand the first pressing. At first, it seems pungently smelly, but once having tasted it, the smell joins the associations of good things to eat. It can be used neat or diluted with vinegar or lemon and a bit of sugar as a salad dressing – delicious – or as the base for a variety of thin dips.

Rice, the mainstay of the Vietnamese diet, comes in dozens of species and styles of preparation: round, ground, perfumed or sticky rice, to name only a few. Simple, steamed white rice is *com* – *com* on a sign, also means 'food', and you see these signs outside modest restaurants. Fried rice is *com rang.*

Pounded young glutinous rice, *com vong,* is a specialty of Vong village, located a few miles north-west of Hanoi. *Com vong* is eaten with bananas and red ripe persimmons. Traditionally, a future son-in-law presented *com* and persimmons to his future parents-in-law. The secret of preparing *com vong* is drying the young rice grains in the frying pan. They are then cooled and pounded in a steady regular rhythm. The *com* flakes are then sieved and spread thinly on lotus leaves.

Square *com* cakes, wrapped in green banana leaves and bound with cords of red bamboo, become wedding cakes. Fillings are well-kneaded ground green beans and strands of coconut. The most famous producer of *com vong* cakes is the Nguyen Ninh family of Hang Than Street and *com vong* cakes are also sold in the confectionery shops of Hang Duong and Hang Dieu Streets.

Rice paper pancakes in the North are called *banh da.*

Flat, white noodles are called *banh pho.*

Clear vermicelli noodles, served in soups, salads or as a side dish, are called *banh hoi* or *bun* in the North. A tasty vermicelli dish, *bun cha,* is a combination of roast pork and fresh herbs served in a tart soup. *Ban thang* is also a vermicelli soup, this time with chicken.

Pork pies, *gio lua,* although eaten throughout Vietnam, originated in Uoc Le village of the former Ha Dong province (just south of Hanoi). Fresh pork is pounded, wrapped in young, yellow banana leaves, then wrapped again in mature banana leaves, the flavour suffusing from the leaves. If you are vaguely surprised at all this pounding and chopping, it must be remembered that as meat, freshly killed, tends to be tough (until recently, Vietnamese kitchens were without refrigeration), so in traditional recipes, it gets pounded, chopped and minced to render it easily chewable!

As they have so much of it, the Vietnamese have excelled themselves in finding innumerable ways of cooking and serving rice. *Banh troi* are marble-sized dumplings made of white rice flour with a rock sugar filling. *Banh chay* are sticky rice cakes containing preserved fruit and bits of lard.

Fresh spring rolls, that is to say, not fried, are called *goi cuon,* which hold a mixture of vermicelli noodles, soy beans, shrimps and mint. Fried spring rolls – a favourite snack – are called *bun nem* in the North.

Another Hanoi specialty is *chao tom,* ground shrimp paste, baked on sugar cane. To eat them, the shrimp paste is scraped off the sugar cane, rolled in rice paper with lettuce, cucumber, coriander and mint and dipped in *ngoc mam.*

When I first came to Hanoi, I used to take lunches with a bunch of Vietnamese colleagues around a big round table. Invariably, there would be a huge bowl of rice; a bowl of water spinach, the ubiquitous green vegetable grown in rivers and streams throughout Vietnam; perhaps another vegetable or tofu; meat of some sort, sometimes meat and fish; always followed by a thin vegetable broth. Although all the dishes were served simultaneously, as they are in restaurants and in Vietnamese homes, rather than in courses, it was invariably the soup the Vietnamese ate last.

Up and down the country, Vietnam has different styles of cuisine, North, Central and South. The North eats more beef and chicken, frogs, eels and snails, as well as seafood and their exotica stretches to dog meat, snakes, crickets, well matured duck embryos, sows' utters and field mice. As most of the latter are considered delicacies, the visitor is highly unlikely to encounter them without making a special effort. The Vietnamese take the pragmatic attitude – if it is nutritious and tastes good, eat it. There is a Vietnamese proverb: 'Learn to eat before learning to speak.'

Dog meat is said to provide extra body heat in winter – and to remove bad luck, if eaten at the end of a lunar month. Snake is the specialty of Le Mat village just outside Hanoi, either cooked or drunk as snake wine *(ruan ran),* which is rice wine embellished with a snake curled up in the bottle. It is said to improve visibility and crucially, male virility. Another delicacy, duck egg embryos *(trung vit long)* are boiled and eaten just before hatching – feathers, bill, webbed feet and all. I cheerfully admit that I have refrained from trying any of these exotica. Hanoi restaurant menus list so many appealing choices that I am still trying to work my way through the irresistible, more recognizable offerings.

One Hanoi dish that cannot go unmentioned is grilled fish, *cha ca.* A certain family has made grilled fish so famous in Cha Ca Street that several family restaurants in the same street have sprung up to compete in serving this specialty.

Another Hanoi specialty, *bun oc,* are huge snails as big as golf balls, boiled and dipped in a strong, fermented shrimp sauce called *nuoc cham,* to be found in a row of restaurants on the south side of West Lake (Ho Tay). *Nuoc cham* sauce requires caution – it is quite pungent.

In Vietnam, particularly in Hanoi, one of the pleasant courtesies is the serving of tea on arrival at any office or in a home, without the host ever offering tea. It is simply assumed that any arrival needs a refreshing cup of tea. Very sensible. In Vietnam, it is green tea, sometimes very strong, sometimes disconcertingly lukewarm, always in cups tinier than those used by Europeans for espresso coffee.

A word to the wise on the subject of coffee, to avoid half-and-half coffee made with overly sweet condensed milk, *ca phe nau,* ask for *ca phe den* – that's the real stuff – good, strong, hot and black. If you want it cold (iced, generally okay in restaurants), ask for *ca phe du.*

While on the subject of drinks, no one can return home and say they have experienced Hanoi without trying fresh draft beer *(bia hoi)* – fresh because it was only made the night before – preferably sitting on a tiny plastic stool at a pavement cafe, a good way to meet the locals. The stronger stuff, rice wine *(xeo),* which tastes a bit like Japanese saki, deserves serious respect and the Vietnamese tend to sling it back in one gulp – 'cent per cent' -- round after round with repeated toasts like lemonade.

For a few treats you will never find at home, head to the shops in Hang Dieu Street that specialize in lotus seed jams, moon cakes and lotus tea, especially just before the Vietnamese New Year *(Tet)*. The smallish market in Ta Hien Street, just north of Hoan Kiem lake, as well as Hanoi's main market, Dong Xuan, are cornucopias of fresh fruit, vegetables, herbs you've never seen before and much else: oranges of several varieties and colours, limes, huge pamplemousse (unsour grapefruit), mangoes, both large and very tiny sweet bananas, papayas, custard apples and in season, longans and lychees, the best in Vietnam, coming from Hai Hung between Hanoi and Haiphong. The lychees are so big, fleshy and succulent that they were formerly offered as tribute to the Chinese imperial court – by demand of the Chinese emperor.

There is one Vietnamese specialty, *banh chung,* traditionally eaten at *Tet* that demands careful consideration.

A long time ago, during the reign of the sixth Hung king (sometime between 700-179BC), the old king decided to hand over the throne to a successor. But which of his heirs should it be? In Vietnam, the line of succession is anything but direct and this seems to have been the case for a very long time. A genie (spirit) suggested to the king that he set his sons a challenge.

'Go anywhere in the world and bring back to me the recipe for the best savoury dish you can find,' the king told his sons, which testifies to the lengthy gourmet tradition of Vietnam.

The princes set out in all directions in greater or lesser state, depending upon age and rank. Sadly, the king's motherless sixteenth son, Lang Lieu, watched the departure of his wealthy brothers. Having neither servants nor advisers, what was he to do? One night, a genie came to him in a dream.

'Nothing is more precious than rice,'said the genie. 'Therefore, take sticky rice, clean it in clear water and steam it, then make two loaves. One should be round like heaven in gratitude for its help, the other square, as everyone knows, the shape of the earth. Inside, put mung beans ground with a mortar, lard and minced meat with green onions. Then stew it for a day and a night. Trust my words,' said the genie and disappeared.

When he awoke, Prince Lang Lieu went to find his old nurse and told her his dream. Together, she helped him to make the cakes and after much practice, he learned to do it himself. When the long awaited day came for the brothers to put their dishes before the king, they brought exotic fruits, spices and strange unknown fish from foreign lands. The old king tasted each of their dishes, taking the opinions of his courtiers – and chose the sticky rice cakes of the sixteenth son.

He not only approved of the symbolic shapes of the round and square cakes, but appreciated the far-sighted common sense the prince had demonstrated in having relied on foods that were easy to hand. When the king asked Lang Lieu how he had come to offer the rice cakes, the prince told him about the genie in the dream. From this revelation, the king realised that Lang Lieu already had heavenly approval and felt happily confirmed in his choice of successor. As for the cakes, the king had the recipe distributed throughout the land and decreed that the round cake should be called *banh day,* the square cake *banh chung.*

I wonder if Prince Lang Lieu made a good king. He must have died a fat one.

The square cakes with which I had two sticky encounters, are shaped in a wooden mould eight or nine inches square and wrapped in banana leaves to steam, which gives the rice a ghoulish, green tinge and does nothing nice for the taste – the least appealing Vietnamese food I have ever eaten. Delectable, they are not. I cannot imagine how the Hung king found them to his taste, not even helped down with sips of strong rice wine.

The first time I encountered *banh chung* was at a gathering of retired puppeteers. The second time was at a *Tet* party in my mini-hotel for two of the staff, departing for their villages before the holidays. A thick wedge was placed in my bowl and my *Viet kieu* (Vietnamese living overseas) friend genially joshed, 'Go ahead, they are all waiting to laugh.' Put like that, how could I refuse? Doubtless, watching me wrestle with chopsticks to 'cut off' a bit of sticky *banh chung* must have been the funniest thing since Mickey Mouse, judging from the suppressed giggles.

It is easy to avoid *banh chung* with reputedly at least five hundred traditional dishes to choose from. Having said that, Vietnamese food comes highly recommended, not least because it always looks so appetising, unsurprising when there is a proverb: 'A dish should be a treat to the eye first, before being delicious.'

As the Vietnamese eat rice at home in one form or another, morning, noon and night, there is also another infamous proverb: 'When you tire of rice (at home with your wife), take *pho*' (eat out, take a mistress).

TRADITIONAL WATER PUPPETS

Money can even buy fairies!
– Vietnamese proverb

No visitor to Hanoi should miss seeing the water puppets, unique to Vietnam. At first I thought they were toys, the chubby wooden dolls peering through the windows of souvenir shops in Hanoi. Their cheery, painted faces and plump little bodies are very untypical of the Vietnamese. What's more, they float! At Thang Long Water Puppet Theatre at the north end of Hoan Kiem Lake, they go into action.

The theatre darkens to a glittering red satin floating palace. Green bamboo blinds serve as curtains behind the watery stage. Drums roll, wooden knockers knock, cymbals crash and a female singer belts out a piercing screech. Before I can wonder how she produces such a noise, presto, shiny gilt dragons pop up from beneath the surface of the water, spewing spouts of water. They bob up and down, dragon-like I suppose, swimming back and forth across the stage. Quite a flamboyant entrance.

A farmer riding a black and white buffalo emerges from between the green bamboo blinds, ploughing watery furrows. Another farmer appears, flipping water with a tiny basket from one paddy to another, while another deftly plants sprigs of rice. Astonishing! How do they manage to make floating puppets do that? The fifteen inch (38 cm) high puppets are so comical that it is easy to forget that they are being dexterously manipulated from behind the bamboo blinds by strings passed through lengthy, underwater poles.

In the next scene, lotus pads appear and virtuoso butterflies flit about as a fisherman is chased by an assertive fish. A tidy line of ducks are herded by a Vietnamese hunk, flinging a net, head-shaking worriedly as a tiger swims nearer and nearer. The hunk makes to protect a fair damsel from the tiger, or perhaps it is the fair damsel who chases the tiger up a palm tree. But up the palm tree shoots the tiger, somehow manipulated from below.

Kids from six to sixty love it, no common language required. This is pure slapstick, albeit extremely skilful slapstick. Next from his boat, the fisherman does battle with an enormous shiny red fish, the victory easily won by the fish. The fisherman falls oars over head into the water and swims very comically, stiff wooden arm over wooden arm, with the fish on his back. In a few minutes the fisherman recovers himself, this time fishing placidly with a round basket that he drops by mistake over the head of a pretty pearl fisher. How the audience loves it.

In the next scene, a gang of young boys lark about in the water as boys will, turning somersaults and with incredible expertise on the part of the puppeteers, one boy is tossed onto the shoulders of another, then another, to make a stack of three boys!

At the sound of a chime, sparklers go off under water, making sparks and smoke. From the smoke, eight dancing girls emerge, flapping their angel wings. I later learn that this is a scene from a famous Chinese legend in which two students each marry a fairy, a story incorporated by the Vietnamese into a popular folk opera *(cheo)* that originated in villages of the North.

The finale features the four sacred creatures: turtle, dragon, phoenix and unicorn, amidst much smoke and sparklers. The music – flute, lute, two-string fiddle, a loud horn, drums, gong and a wailing singer – create a boisterous din throughout.

While the audience is still clapping and rocking with laughter and delight, the bamboo blinds rise and the ten men and women puppeteers step forward, hip-deep in water to take a bow.

You might easily imagine that water puppetry is a recent diversion dreamt up for the tourists. In fact, it is a traditional folk art going back for certain to the twelfth century and very probably, much earlier to the rural villages of the North where it originated. An inscription on a stone stele at the Doi pagoda (Tien District, Nam Ha Province), confirms that water puppetry was already in vogue as a court entertainment in 1121 under Emperor Ly Nhan Tong.

Village festivals in Vietnam – the heavy festival season is in April – are lively events including boat-racing, wrestling, giant swings, competitive kite-flying, bird-racing, firecrackers (until they were banned) and water puppetry, performed in village ponds. In a rice culture, ponds are laboriously dug by hand to raise the floor level for houses against the heavy flooding of monsoon rains and the water that fills the ponds is used for cultivation and daily use. Naturally, there is a homely proverb: 'When drinking water, remember its source.'

The structures of most water puppet theatres are temporary, erected for festivals. The oldest permanent water puppet pavilion, still standing, built in the later Le dynasty (1533-1708), is at Thay pagoda (Quoc Oai, Son Tay Province). Another dating from 1775, remains intact at the Dong temple in Hanoi.

Architecturally, water puppet theatres have three parts: a manipulation room behind the bamboo blinds, a stage (the pond water or a water tank) and the audience. Traditionally, the performances were given in daylight and the village pond might have tufts of grass, water manioc or clumps of duckweed or water hyacinth growing and floating among the puppets to make manipulation just that bit more difficult.

The puppets are carved from light, durable wood, often from fig trees and stand twelve to thirty-nine inches (30-99 cm) tall and weigh from two to ten pounds (1-6 kg). The base of the puppet is submerged and fitted with a control mechanism that serves as a float. They are coated with resin from the lacquer tree and painted bright colours from plant resins. The manipulation poles are of wood or bamboo and measure ten to thirteen feet (3-4 m) long. Movements of the puppets are controlled by fine strings made of waxed, plaited hair, coir, silk or jute strung through the poles.

Puppet carving ranks as an important folk art and is similar both in form and subject matter to the carvings found in communal houses *(dinh)* of the seventeenth and eighteenth centuries: fish, frogs, dragons, foxes, snakes.

The characters in water puppet sketches are borrowed from history, legends and myths as well as from peasant daily life – planting rice, catching crabs, fishing, tending ducks, chasing a fox, ploughing – activities with which peasants would readily identify as well as admiring the skill of the puppeteers.

Sometimes snippets of stories from classical opera *(tuong)* or folk opera *(cheo)* are lifted. Such is the case of the *Delivery of the Prince in his Palanquin* and the *Severing of Khuon Ling Ta's Head* from the *tuong* play, *Son Hai*. The *Xich Binh Fire Fight* is taken from the *tuong* play, *The Three Warring States.*

The *Fairy's Sighting of Tu Thuc,* is taken from a *cheo* play based on a legend in which the hero, Tu Thuc, lives with a fairy for three years, then returns Rip van Winkle style to find the world much older and tragically for a Vietnamese, himself forgotten in his own village.

Sometimes scenes and stories intentionally get mixed up in the staging to add an element of surprise for the audience. Fishing from peasant life might blend into the story of Le Loi sailing on Hoan Kiem lake when the golden turtle reclaims the sacred sword. The scene, *Felling Banana Trees,* can unexpectedly evolve into the *Severing of Lieu Thang's Head.* Sketches run up to seven minutes. The rhyming texts, spoken and sung, identify the stories, poetry or folk songs for Vietnamese audiences. But originally, water puppetry was purely a mime form.

Traditionally, water puppetry was practiced as a hobby, although village puppetry guilds have also acted as mutual-aid societies. Ponds were used for rearing fish as well as for performances. Not all guild members perform. However, all guild members contribute rice and money towards a fund to be handed down from generation to generation.

Historically, few women performed. Guild members tended to be heads of families and women were considered not strong enough to manipulate the poles. The women of Thang Long troupe disprove this supposed frailty. More crucially, women were considered poor security risks as it was feared they would divulge how the puppet mechanisms worked, if they moved as brides to their husbands' villages.

Until very recently, guarding professional secrets has restricted the possibility of an exchange of skills. Although some stories are popular and enacted by nearly every guild, each guild had to reinvent the techniques, resulting in a diversity of forms. In the past, puppetry was learned through imitation and practice, the old teaching the young. Currently, Hanoi has four guilds: Dao Thuc, Nhan Thai, Ha Huong and Thi Lan.

Probably the most universally beloved water puppet character is Teu, the round-tummied, fun-loving, mischievous, jokey master of ceremonies, who makes irreverent comments and jokes, something the Vietnamese throughout their long history of domination – Chinese, feudal, French, Communist – have often been denied.

Of the water puppet troupes, the Thang Long company of Hanoi is best known, having performed nearly round the world. Some years ago during a tour to the US, members of the troupe were moved to tears at Lincoln Centre in New York when the mayor raised the flag of Viet Nam before an audience of foreign diplomats. In 1997, the troupe toured U.S. universities. It seems to me ironic that the Thang Long water puppets got to the University of Kansas before London in 1998.

So popular are the performances abroad that stages have been left, one in Europe, one in America. Yet the company has known hard times. Founded during the Vietnam War in 1969 without a theatre, just a meeting room in a thatched house, the troupe gave only one or two performances a week, always at a loss.

Le Van Ngo, director of the Thang Long Company, greets me in his top floor office above the theatre, a man of indeterminate age with black hair and lively dark eyes in a serious, kindly face. He admits that he was over twenty before he learned to manipulate water puppets. He had not come from a family of puppeteers, but joined a water puppet troupe as a singer. During performances, he saw 'how much the children liked the puppets and found love for the puppets' himself.

He recalled the difficult days of 1985, when not only Thang Long Water Puppet Theatre, but the entire country was on the brink of financial collapse and starvation. The Hanoi Cultural Service agreed to sponsor the troupe, providing capital and facilities and most importantly, guaranteeing to pay minimal wages to the artists. Success was not sudden, but built gradually by hard work through many ups and downs. Since 1993, the theatre has run almost without sponsorship, except that the city still pays a small portion of the puppeteers' salaries. Le Van Ngo is immensely proud that the Thang Long troupe is the only theatre in Vietnam that performs three hundred sixty-five days a year and the only cultural activity that earns a profit (apart from the circus). And he is also immensely pleased that his artists can afford to live on their earnings, rare in Vietnam. Most people have to moonlight to supplement the earnings from their jobs.

To join the Thang Long troupe, puppeteers go through a four-year course at the College of Arts, then serve an apprenticeship with a troupe in one of three villages (Chua Thai, Nam Chan, Nguyen Xa). To recruit puppeteers, they place commercials on television, but only high school graduates, residents of Hanoi may apply. First, they must pass an examination in the theatre to test their ear for music and their ability to perform. Then they must pass a second entrance examination at the college.

These days there are twenty-four puppeteers, two full troupes that alternate performances, sometimes one touring. A troupe is made up of ten puppeteers plus two assistants, six musicians plus a music assistant, a lighting person and a director. The troupe is no longer made up of family members, but 'members must be from the village of Hanoi.' The artists range in age from twenty to fifty, 'two or three generations.'

The puppets are replaced every three years.

'Puppets are made by the artisans. We have two or three troupes of puppets in store. They change very little.'

Nowadays, about half of the three hundred seats are filled by Vietnamese, a sign that foreign approbation can rekindle enthusiasm for indigenous culture. As my Swedish friend who attended a performance with me, put it, 'Who could resist the water puppets? They are irresistible.'

It isn't until I ask Le Van Ngo about the character of Teu that his face really lights up.

'Teu acts as a master of ceremonies, he always opens the performance. What he says changes, he makes social commentary. Even if it is a tragedy, Teu makes it bearable by making it funny.'

'I can see that you love Teu.'

'And my puppeteers.'

A few days later I am invited to a gathering of retired puppeteers.

I have never seen a cricket dancing – nor playing a flute for that matter! This is quite a large cricket wearing a smart, cut-away tailcoat with a mischievous gleam in his painted eye. He has leapt from the pages of a Vietnamese children's fable onto the stage of the recently formed *Union International de la Marionette Vietnam,* a club for retired puppeteers. Its guiding spirit and founder, Nguyen Huy Hong, in whose house and garden the club meets, is a lively, retired puppeteer with flowing grey hair, who feels it a personal mission to alert Vietnam's veteran puppeteers to the urgency of passing on their skills to younger puppeteers before they shuffle off to the heavenly stage.

141

A water puppet theatre has been built in Hong's garden on the bank of the To Lich river in Hanoi's suburbs, beside which a small museum contains a crowd of ageing puppets and two thousand books on puppetry.

As the cricket dances his jig, a boy behind me with a cast on his leg, taps his crutch to the rhythm. The tiniest toddlers sit in the front rows, their almond eyes wide with pleasure. Larger children, ranging from eight to eighty, sit in plastic chairs surrounded by overflow spectators, standing. Still more people peer down from windows, stairs and balconies.

Naturally, being a Vietnamese gathering, it began with much hand-shaking, card exchanges and tiny cups of tea served around low tables under fruit trees. But it wasn't long before we got down to serious puppeteering, half the audience enraptured, the unsmiling professionals watching critically.

First off were the water puppets, buffalo boys, an iridescent gilt fish, a fox that ran up a tree with a duck in his mouth and boatmen rocking gently in their boats as they rowed, a boy and girl singing folk ditties *(quan ho)* back and forth to one another, boat to boat.

In the front row a tiny tot got so excited that he tipped forward out of his plastic chair and almost fell into the pond. I am told that many a child has slid down a slippery bank into the village pond while watching water puppets. A woman with long grey hair sitting beside me sang along with the singers and she whispered that she used to sing professionally.

The next performer was a scantily clad Cham temple dancer, a wooden marionette, who thanks to the numerous strings attached to the puppeteer's hat, shoulders, belt, hands, every finger and even his feet, executed a beguilingly graceful, finger-rippling dance, the black shadow of the puppeteer mirroring her actions in full view behind her.

Had I not seen the next act assembled, I would never have believed it. Two female puppeteers placed ruffled ballet *tutus* on their heads, covering their faces and bent forward over a table, their bare arms becoming legs. Two more puppeteers donned a long white satin-sleeved glove on one arm to form a curved neck. Red beaks and eyes at their fingertips became the heads of swans – dancing *Swan Lake,* what else? And a very convincing performance it was, too, learned from Eastern Bloc puppeteers.

142

Turning our chairs front to back, the audience now faced a small, purple-curtained opening like a Punch and Judy stage, where a fuzzy rabbit, his friend the bumble bee and a whingeing wolf appeared – Russian hand puppets.

'I'm so tired and hungry,' whined the wolf. 'I have such a hunger for a little rabbit!'

Naturally, the wolf caught the rabbit in a wolf-hug and the poor rabbit squealed, bringing the bee to his rescue. The bee, attached to a springy wire, set about stinging the wolf until the wolf let go of the rabbit and keeled over. Then came the stealthy approach of the bee and the rabbit to the carcass of the wolf.

'Is he dead? Is he really dead? Is he really, really dead?'

The Vietnamese children responded with *da, da, da,* (yes, yes, yes). Imagine my surprise after the applause to discover that the puppeteer was none other than the grey-haired lady who had been singing along beside me.

After a jigging cricket and three sequined dancers from the Central Highlands, string puppets, we settled to sipping tiny cups of extremely strong rice wine – at ten a.m.! The cinnamon-flavoured peanuts just about kept my words coherent, maybe.

The rest of the day was spent feet up.

CLASSICAL AND FOLK OPERA

It is easier to speak well than to act well
– Vietnamese proverb

As a fairly indiscriminate lover of European opera, I was thrilled some time ago when the scholar, Huu Ngoc, invited me to accompany him to a performance of Vietnamese classical opera *(tuong)*. As a preliminary, he introduced me to the then assistant director of the Northern Tuong Theatre in Hanoi, Mrs Nguyen Thi Nhung, a chic woman of a certain age. How had she trained for *tuong,* I asked?

'I competed nationally to obtain a place at the Stage School. The year I applied, only thirty students were chosen from 1,300 applicants. Training for the classical theatre – singing, dancing and learning the repertoire – required four years. I entered Stage School at fourteen, just after the outbreak of war and attended from 1964 to 1968' – during the Vietnam War – not a very auspicious time for entering the arts or for much else in Vietnam.

'Having completed my studies, I was appointed to the Northern Tuong Theatre, the national opera company, which had been evacuated to a country site eleven miles (17 km) from Hanoi. The troupe was divided into small groups of seven or eight, and larger groups of fifteen to twenty and sent touring round the countryside, sleeping in village houses, giving performances for peasants in village halls and in army hospitals.'

I knew that the popular musical folk opera *(cheo)* had originated in villages of the North and that musical Renovated Theatre *(cai luong)* had originated more recently around Ho Chi Minh City, adding spoken dialogue. Not wanting to ask an indelicate question – had Vietnamese opera derived from China – I ask how long *tuong* had been performed in Vietnam.

'There are two schools of classical opera in Vietnam, that of the North, *gua ming,* and that of the South around Hue, *hat boi. Tuong* is based on mythical, epic, heroic and tragic themes.'

Then Mrs Nguyen volunteered, 'It is difficult to explain with any precision the differences between Chinese and Vietnamese classical opera. Obviously, Vietnamese *tuong* owes much to the tradition of classical Chinese opera. It is known for certain that in the fourteenth century, following the Vietnamese victory over the Chinese, that an excellent Chinese opera singer, dancer and actor, Ly Nguyen Cat, was captured by the Vietnamese Tran dynasty and that he taught classical opera in the royal harem.'

I couldn't help wondering if he had to become a eunuch, but couldn't quite bring myself to ask Mrs Nguyen through the distinguished scholar, Huu Ngoc, as interpreter.

It must be said of any borrowed art form or craft in Vietnam, be it lacquer, sericulture, painting, porcelain, whatever, once the Vietnamese have inculcated the skills, the craft becomes Vietnamised, Vietnam being a nation of irrepressible creators. Classical *tuong,* therefore, would have evolved into something quite Vietnamese.

'No serious research has yet been done into the earliest origins of classical opera in Vietnam. According to some historians, small plays and sketches began to appear in the tenth century, long before the capture of Ly Nguyen Cat.

'But it is generally acknowledged that the real flowering of the form occurred under the Nguyen dynasty in Hue in the nineteenth century and the best known *tuong* composer of that period was Dao Tan.'

Although formerly every village had its troupe of amateur *tuong* players who performed at village festivals, *tuong* has suffered in recent years from the onslaught of western pop music.

Having a penchant for being on time, I was pleased when Huu Ngoc suggested that we start half an hour before the performance, only a few minutes walk away. As the performance was to be given by members of the newly formed Stage Club of Vietnam, sponsored by Press and Radio of Vietnam, it was taking place in the auditorium of Radio Vietnam. We arrived fifteen minutes early to a full house, but I had not reckoned on the esteem enjoyed by Huu Ngoc. We were led smartly to the front row where five empty seats remained, reserved for dignitaries.

Very sensibly as it was summer, Vietnamese men were wearing open-necked, short-sleeved shirts. The women were elegant in flowing *ao dais.* Directly across from us was a bald-headed man with a straggly beard – a dead ringer for Ho Chi

Minh. No one took the least notice of him. I was the only foreigner in the room.

The performance began with drum rolls and a gong, the orchestra made up of a two-string fiddle, long-necked and moon-shaped guitars, a bamboo flute, a bowl-shaped gong and my favourite instrument, the one-string, sorrowful-sounding *dan bau,* which often carries the melody. Oddly, it sounds vaguely like a cor anglais.

A man and a woman sang in unison to the accompaniment of a flute and wood-knockers. An aria, perhaps? Certainly, this was not the opera performance I had expected.

Then a female singer, flashing red and silver sequins, placed a brass tray holding red cellophane-wrapped parcels and candles on a low table. Huu Ngoc whispered that she was a medium, part of the cult of holy mothers – the skies, the sea and the mountains. Four pretty girls wearing glittering red headbands, green sashes over pink tunics and black trousers entered, singing and dancing, waving their lacy fans. They handed the medium two wooden sticks and her movements looked like rowing. Then the medium removed the silvery tunic and earrings – was this to be a striptease? – to reveal a long-sleeved white satin blouse and trousers. She slipped into a yellow jacket, a yellow hat and a turquoise sash – a costume change on stage.

'The cult of the spirits,' whispered Huu Ngoc. The girls danced, bowing and kneeling. Having finished with the oars, the medium was handed two wooden swords and the dance began to look like riding on horseback. The attendants brought out teacups and danced tipsily from side to side in a graceful rendition of drunkenness. Then the medium took up a basket full of flower petals and scattered them into the laps of the musicians.

Off came the yellow jacket and the hat, to be replaced by two enormous silver rings around her neck, an embroidered orange headdress, a gold shirt and a glittering green brocade jacket. She placed the tray of red parcels on her head and danced, turning, kneeling and rising. The four attendants reappeared carrying candles and lotus blossoms and the medium handed out the red cellophane-wrapped triangular parcels to those of us in the front row. But was this *tuong?*

'Dried sugar rice flour cake for the cult. You can eat it,' whispered Huu Ngoc.

146

A dazzling lady from the Voice of Vietnam Radio – obviously a personality, wearing a shocking pink *ao dai* with clouds on the sleeves and a glittering procession of peasants under parasols marching diagonally from hip to hem – explained that the club had been founded at a moment when the theatre was in decline, in an attempt to revive it. Her *ao dai* alone should do the trick.

'There are fewer and fewer performances, because few people understand the performances,' she explained. Surely a few talks on Vietnam Radio would help, or a few documentaries with commentary on VN-TV?

The next performer was a female singer wearing a dazzling splash of colours. Her song was exceedingly anguished, almost unbearably poignant.

'She has been betrayed by her lover,' whispered Huu Ngoc.

Next, a beautiful girl with wild eyes hopped onto the stage in a sitting position 'riding a horse.' She turned cartwheels and walked on her knees, then knelt as though she were looking at her reflection in a pond.

This one I was prepared for, a famous *tuong* story in which the heroine is a fox, who it has taken a thousand years to attain 'the essence of becoming human.' But she has been betrayed by her lover and is fearful that as punishment, she will lose her 'human essence'.

As she peered at her reflection, I swear, her nostrils started to twitch. Her eyes narrowed and she became fox-like, her fingers curling into claws, her wrists bending outward and she seemed to discover fur growing on her forearms. Meanwhile, her face contorted and seemed quite transformed. She kept trying to pry her fingers straight and to remove the fur. The dance ended in a wailing lament, the mournful howl of a fox on a hilltop. A brilliant performance.

'There are Confucian implications,' whispered Huu Ngoc, but he left it at that. Simplistic moral of story: choose your lover very carefully. As a complete change of pace, we then had a romantic ballad, sung by a singer in an *ao dai* to challenge *Joseph's Technicolour Dream Coat.*

'She is a well-known singer.'

But was it *tuong?* I was ill prepared for what came next.

Onto the stage strode a muscular young man wearing – a boa constrictor! It became instantly clear that we had had our dose of

147

tuong for the evening. The new club organisers were taking no chances that the audience would go away bored. Despite the billing of classical opera, we were to be treated to a right royal Vietnamese variety show. So taking the view that everyone loves a circus, they had brought on the circus.

I didn't mind watching the strong man wrap his enormous snake around his neck, over his shoulders and around his thighs. I became a little uneasy when a female assistant with a somewhat smaller boa constrictor joined him and climbed up onto his bent knee to do a high kick. Then another boa constrictor appeared and the young man became a snake-stand for two snakes, plus the girl and her snake, of course. I began to wonder how heavy boa constrictors are, the big ones.

Eventually, the girl piled her snake onto the gallant young man and oops – he was heading for the audience. My rapid exit was physically and diplomatically blocked by the directrice of the circus to whom I had just been introduced, sitting beside me. Perhaps she didn't like boa constrictors either, for to my relief, the snake man headed towards two young boys who looked as if they would just love to say hello to a big snake.

The rest of the evening consisted of a couple of clowns, *'cheo',* said Huu Ngoc, followed by wooden puppet temple dancers, two radio actors reading gags about television commercials, two comedians who reminded me of Britain's *Two Ronnies,* a poet who turned out to have painted the stage backdrop and a seven-year-old girl in a peasant costume singing *I Am A Rebel from Binh Minh* – interminably. Eventually, she was dragged off stage and at last, came a farewell folk song entitled *Don't Leave.* We, and the rest of the relieved audience, left.

Huu Ngoc's first words were, 'What time is it?'

Half past ten is a very late performance in Hanoi. As we walked back towards Tran Hung Dao Street, a ding-donging vehicle approached and liberally sprayed the street – and both of us from the knees down – with water.

It felt like three in the morning.

(It is still not possible to see full-length performances of *tuong* in Hanoi, but happily, these days the National Tuong Company has its own theatre at 51 Duong Thanh and gives one-hour 'taster' performances. They begin with ceremonial Great Court Music (drums, flutes, symbols and wooden 'bells'), followed by Small Court Music, traditional flag-waving and from *tuong,* the magnificent fox scene described above as well as a very comical and acrobatic scene in which an arrogant young blade tries to woo the young wife of an elderly gentleman. The costumes are superb and the performances bewitching. Check days and times: www.vietnamtuongtheatre.com)

However entranced I was by *tuong,* it must be admitted that the truest, purest indigenous Vietnamese theatrical art form is *cheo,* the folk opera born of village festivals. Going back to the eleventh century in the Red River Delta of the North, *cheo* matured in the fifteenth and sixteenth centuries, reaching its peak in the seventeenth and eighteenth. A recurrent theme is the sad fate of women under feudalism.

Unlike *tuong,* which extols the epic deeds of the aristocracy, *cheo* describes the life of ordinary people, giving voice to farmers' aspirations in a feudal society. Like *tuong,* it is an art form combining speech, singing, dancing and music to tell a story. The majority of the nearly two hundred original *cheo* melodies originates from folk songs. Goodness inevitably wins out in *cheo's* moral messages, reflecting the benevolence of Buddhism and the virtues of Confucianism, which is not to say that they are not full of satire and raucous humour.

Unlike *tuong,* although the stories and plots are well known, performers of *cheo* may improvise in the songs, modifying the melodies, adding words to fit the occasion. Plays run without acts or intervals and may be extended or cut, depending upon the inspiration of the performers or the response of an audience. This does not mean that performances are undisciplined. A Vietnamese audiences will recognise instantly if a performer has assumed a 'metal', 'earth' or 'copper' voice, telling them about the character.

Instruments used to accompany *cheo* include small and larger two-stringed fiddles, the *ho* and the *nhi,*; the bamboo flute *(sao)* and percussion, which plays a major role. The drums include a small drum, a large drum, a horizontal cylindrical drum, a gong and wooden 'tocsin' *(mo).* An old saying, 'There can be no *cheo* without a drum,' explains rather succinctly the importance of the drums and it is said that good drumming can make up for an otherwise weak performance.

Although there are hundreds of *cheo* plays, only seven are recognised as classics. Vietnamese audiences know them so well that the characters have become figures of speech in Vietnamese daily life: the jealous wife, the good woman, the unfaithful wife, the drunken man, deaf teachers, wealthy men, prime ministers, students, flirtatious women and buffoons.

Having read in *Heritage,* Vietnam Airlines' magazine, that there were performances of *cheo* in Hanoi, I was determined to see it. One evening, I set out with a *Viet kieu* couple (overseas Vietnamese), staying at my hotel. We arrived at the Traditional Arts Theatre (15 Nguyen Dinh Chieu Street) ten minutes late to find that the performance of the Cheo Circle was packed out. Although there was an overflow of people standing at the doorway peering in, as visitors from abroad, we were kindly bustled inside. My new friend Lin dropped her shoes, I followed her example although it was freezing cold. We were motioned to sit on a straw mat in front of the rows of chairs with the children. The children were wearing leather jackets, woollen leggings, but had kicked off their sandals. After some shifting to make sure that the children could see, the performance began with the master of ceremonies, doubtless, saying what an auspicious occasion it was and how good it was to see so many people

The hotel receptionist who inquired had told us that tickets would cost $4. At the door, we had been bustled inside, probably because it was late and my friends were Vietnamese and therefore admitted free.

At centre stage, an altar covered by a red cloth held two brass candlesticks and a large brass incense burner. Tall, red lacquer candlesticks stood like standard lamps on each side of the altar. A handful of burning joss sticks had been stuck into a pyramid of mandarin oranges on a lower table.

The first performer was a female singer seated on a mat between a guitar player and a thin elderly man with a tiny drum – a *H'at A Dao* singer. I am sure I recognised them from a Folk Music Club evening. This was decidedly not *cheo*. The epic, sung in a minor key, seemed to be a lament and the audience continued to chatter throughout. It did rather go on and I was beginning to sympathise when my *Viet kieu* friend, Ang, whispered at the end of the song that the words were a poem written by a poet, highly embarrassed at finding himself in love with a young girl.

Next, three musicians in silk mandarin costumes, carrying a bamboo flute, a two-string fiddle and a moon-shaped guitar, seated themselves to one side of the stage. Four pretty girls in brightly coloured peasant costumes appeared with two rouged clowns, waving paper torches. They sang and danced, using their straw hats to form a synchronised, moving circle. Next came a flirtatious female singer, who used a fan to vivacious effect, followed by a male crooner, his tenor voice heavy with vibrato.

A grand personage in a scarlet velvet mandarin tunic, flashing gold and silver sequins, strode onto the stage. The embroidered dragon head spreading across his tummy was especially riveting, his ensemble completed by a pair of turned-up-toed boots and a blue cloth band tied around his head. He carried a red rod with yellow silk tassels in each hand and stamped deliberately about the stage in his boots, singing gustily.

'Performing a ceremony,' whispered Ang. At one point, the mandarin balanced precariously on one foot with the other held high, bent at the knee. Everyone clapped, presumably his balance.

Suddenly, the master of ceremonies, wearing a white business suit, burst into song and took on the character of 'an emperor,' whispered Ang.

The following number had us all shrieking with laughter. A beautiful princess had obviously set her sights on her humble lute teacher. The flamboyant princess dressed in royal yellow, carried an ostrich-feather fan and flirted outrageously with the poor tutor, a strikingly handsome young man, who looked extremely discomforted by the whole procedure, as well he might, not only in fear of losing his job, but rather more importantly, his head, if the emperor were to discover this highly dangerous game.

At first, the princess sat on her red velvet stool, flirting demurely from behind her fan. The young man sang a sorrowful song and she gazed at him appealingly. He refused even to glance at her. Her next ploy was to drop her fan at his feet. He did not pick it up, so rather irritably, she picked it up herself. Not to be rebuffed, she approached him from behind and touched his shoulder. He leapt up off his stool as though he'd had an electric shock and crossed the stage to another stool.

The princess pursued him, threw her arms around him and tried to sit on his lap. Highly alarmed, he leapt up again and strode off, the princess following in hot pursuit with her stool, which she placed very close to his. The princess then became more determined. She placed her fan in her teeth to leave her hands free and approached him from behind, touching his neck. He leapt away again. She twirled in front of him and ended by kneeling at his feet. Apprehensively, he moved off again and she lunged at him, finally catching him by the arm. Steadfastly throughout, he had never stopped singing.

Now she held onto his arm and dragged him to one side of the stage, then caught him by the shoulders. Meekly, he held up the last three fingers of one hand, as she curled her fingers triumphantly over his, one, two, and three.

Finally, in desperation, he tried to beat her off, this time with the lute. She wrested it away from him and flung the lute angrily to the floor. With an anguished face, weeping, the tutor knelt to pick up his broken instrument as the princess laughed bitterly. The audience adored every minute of it.

'Cheo,' whispered Ang, obviously enraptured.

The finale was a medley of folk songs, the stage full of singing peasants. I shall never forget the beautiful, impassioned, frustrated princess.

(Cheo performances occur occasionally in Hanoi, given by the Cheo Folk Circle and the Vietnam Cheo Theatre Company. Watch *Vietnam News* for notices of performances, but ask a Vietnamese to confirm by telephone.)

152

REFORM THEATRE – *CAI LUONG*

Girls look for talent, boys for beauty
– Vietnamese proverb

The little Golden Bell *cai luong* theatre at the corner of Hang Bac and Ta Hien – when it's open – offers highly amusing, farcical entertainment, falling somewhere between Gilbert and Sullivan, American musicals and German operettas. Easily understood without a word of Vietnamese, *cai luong,* known as Reform Theatre, has nothing to do with politics, although some of the historical plots criticise feudalism in a general way. But there are also more modern plots that comment on contemporary life. In this instance, 'reform' merely means 'renovated theatre' as opposed to *cheo,* the older form of folk opera still performed at village festivals.

Historically, *cai luong* theatre was an outgrowth of *cheo,* musical folk theatre that originated in villages of the North. *Cai luong* originated as recently as a century ago in the South around the Mekong delta, borrowing a few lines of spoken dialogue from French drama, spliced between the singing.

All aspects of the theatre are represented in *cai luong:* satire, comedy, tragedy, domestic drama, literature, and I was told by a director of the Golden Bell Theatre that it would require a connoisseur to recognise the difference in some instances between *cheo* and *cai luong.*

Until recently, both *cheo* and *cai luong* were popular with the people and there were performances of *cai luong* every night. But during the last few years, since television and videos brought pop music to Vietnam's young and Chinese soap operas on TV to the old, *cai luong* has lost ground to television, discos and karaoke. Since 1990, performances have become less and less frequent. The Golden Bell Theatre keeps going – just – on support from the city of Hanoi. The meagre salaries (not enough to live on which seems to be the norm for many employees) of the fifty of so actors, musicians and theatre workers, are paid by the government. The government also covers the cost of one new production each year.

When I first came to Hanoi, I was lucky to attend a *cai luong* performance of an adaptation of Vietnam's great epic poem, *The Tale of Kieu*. It was written by the country's most illustrious poet, Nguyen Du, who in Vietnam enjoys no less esteem and respect than Shakespeare in the West. Kieu scholars endlessly debate the Vietnamese concepts of *tai* (talents and gifts from the gods) and *menh* (fate) and how the latter thwarts the former, how the talented and gifted are doomed by fate.

Simplistically, Kieu is the Vietnamese *Romeo and Juliet,* the story of star-crossed lovers, so deeply embedded in the Vietnamese psyche that it has been said that one cannot possibly understand the Vietnamese unless he or she understands *Kieu*. The poem has even come to be used rather like the Bible in that a Vietnamese will let the pages of *Kieu* fall open as a stroke of fate to guide him in decision-making. Naturally, with that kind of a recommendation, I read the poem in translation and wept in sympathy with the sufferings of the pure-hearted heroine, Kieu – as well as marvelling at the poetry (in the English translation by Michael Counsell).

I had even gone so far as to suggest, only half in jest, to a member of the Writers' Association that they should make a movie of *Kieu* and export it to the West, after which, every romantic from Prague to Patagonia would have to visit Vietnam. A film of *Kieu* would leave *Indochine* sinking in a basket boat. From reading the poem, I knew that there was plenty of drama in the plot to make it easy to follow, with or without the poetic dialogue, unfortunate though it would be to miss the poetry.

What I did not know was that a performance of *Kieu* does rather go on – for three hours without an interval – so it was a bit like sending an opera novice to Wagner's *Gottedammerung* as an introduction to opera. The curtain went up on a silky backdrop with a silhouette of weeping willows. Instant theatrical magic. My heart went slightly faint at the first sounds of music, an overly-loud onslaught of flute and high-pitched, very Oriental soprano. The five-tone scale can strike terror in the ear of any Westerner on first impact and the smallish Cai Luong Theatre was awash with it, every nook and cranny.

154

The first character to appear on stage was a quintessentially Vietnamese heart throb in the form of a long finger-nailed young man (to prove that he was a gentleman and did no physical work). He wore rouge, lipstick and false eyelashes, a rhinestone bedecked headdress and a green silk glittering tunic over flowing white trousers. To add to this seeming effeminacy from a Western point of view, he was not only a sugary tenor, but his voice register swooned into the counter-tenor range.

Soon enough the girls come on, a bevy of beauties in white silk, their blue scarves floating through a kind of formation dance. We were left with the lovers Kim and Kieu alone on stage. They sang their romantic duet and pledged their vow of eternal love, recording it on a scroll.

The lights dimmed and the scenery was changed, as all the scenes were changed, without lowering the curtain, thus keeping the action moving.

In the next scene, four bad guys in black and the villain, a moneylender, turned up at Kieu's home. When Kieu's father couldn't pay, amidst the weeping of his dear wife and two daughters, he was led away to prison. Woe upon the family of Kieu. Much weeping and lamenting, the conclusion of which was that Kieu decided that she must somehow save her father – the child's Confucian duty, first and foremost to the parent. But the only precious thing she had to sell to raise money was – herself. Kieu was played by a sweet, sorrowful, innocent-faced, beautiful young girl, of course, wearing white. There was a heart-rending scene with mother and daughter wrapped in one another's arms, which must have moved even the most unsentimental male member of the audience to visions of heroism.

A couple of baddies played the next scene, haggling over the price of Kieu. We knew they were baddies because they flicked their fans angrily at one another (polite Vietnamese never show anger). The female go-between was fat, overly made-up and alternately simpering, charming and nastily ugly, making bad-tempered asides. Her sparing partner in the bargaining, the pimp, looked equally vulgar. *Cai luong* is anything but subtle.

Kieu, of course, could not leave without entrusting the precious scroll to her sister, beseeching her weeping sister to promise to honour her vow of love to Kim in her stead. Another weeping scene – and people on both sides of me had wet eyes –

as Kieu was dragged from her mother's and sister's arms. The acting was superb.

The audience was then given a chance to rein in emotions as the scene switched to the brothel. The lights went up on a grotesque queen of evil, sitting slouched on a couch as a young masseuse lightly pummelled her shoulders. This was the madam of the brothel to which Kieu would be taken.

When Kieu was brought in, the madam greeted her gleefully, greedily gloating on the profits to be made from such a prize. Kieu in her humiliation and distress, drew a knife from within her tunic and stabbed herself. In the *cai luong* dramatization, thankfully, we had been spared Kieu's humiliation at being deflowered by the pimp she had been forced to 'marry'. *Cai luong* is rich in sexual innuendoes, never explicit.

Presently, a man with a kind, open face, wearing a peach-coloured tunic, appeared in the brothel. This was Thuc Sinh, who falls in love with Kieu and buys her out of the brothel. But when he takes her home, his jealous wife Hoan Thu, humiliates Kieu even more, treating her as a servant, demanding that she play her lute and sing, even ordering her to compose poetry. The pain suffered by both Kieu and Thuc Sinh is evident. So well known is this terrible wife in Vietnam, that the name of the character, Hoan Thu, has become synonymous with cunning, wicked wives. And in case you had a modicum of sympathy for the wife, whose husband brought home a second wife right under her nose, in feudal Vietnam husbands had as many wives as they liked – although often the first wife was allowed to choose the second. This guaranteed that the second would be biddable and easily dominated by the first and from the husband's point of view, that the two would get on. At one point in *Kieu,* the terrible wife laments, 'If only he had told me before . . .' suggesting that all might have been so very different.

Poor Kieu, as miserable in Thuc Sinh's house as she had been in the brothel, throws herself in the river, but is rescued by an abbess and taken to a pagoda where we next find her kneeling in the plain brown habit of a novice before an altar. Moments later, Thuc Sinh appears in search of her and tries to convince her to escape. He explains that there is nothing he can do, his wife is so cunning. Unbeknownst to him, his wife has followed him and stands listening from behind one of the pillars. In Confucian, male-dominated Vietnam, the only explanation for this hen pecking that I can imagine is that it must have been the wife who had the money or the connections.

From the pagoda, the drama takes an abrupt leap to a posturing general, resplendent in red and gold velvet, strutting about the stage as only an Oriental general can. It was, however, a trifle difficult to take a general too seriously whose headdress was festooned with springy, red and yellow pompoms and trembling gold medallions. Vietnamese *cai luong* drama – perhaps one should say melodrama – is about as subtle as a silent movie. Feudal characters are held up to ridicule by over-dressing them in outrageously fine costumes and their make-up instantly tells the audience whether the character is good or evil. For this reason, it is easier for a foreigner to follow the plot in *cai luong* than say, certain Italian operas.

The victorious general, despite his ridiculous bobbing pompoms, is the good hero who rescues Kieu and marries her. In the next scene, Kieu is seated beside him, wearing a glittering gold headdress, yellow and white silk, and all those who had made her suffer in the past are brought before her for punishment. The cowering pimp, the madam and the go-between kneel, all begging for mercy. They are quickly dispatched. Only Thuc Sinh, the kind, weak man, who pleads for mercy for his wicked wife, is magnanimously pardoned by Kieu, along with his jealous wife.

At that point the general receives a message from an enemy feudal lord, asking him to negotiate peace. Kieu, longing for peace, pleads with him to negotiate rather than to continue fighting. To please her, the general agrees to meet the enemy. But it is a trap. He is ambushed, first by four soldiers bearing pikes. These he kicks aside in a fine display of *kung fu,* but the nasty feudal lord laughs and the poor brave, betrayed general is no match for the feudal lord's archers. He dies standing, frozen in an attitude of rage, balanced on one foot, the other leg held high, bent at the knee in a brilliant theatrical convention, the position in which Kieu finds him.

Naturally, she is distraught and the lament she sings is no less heart-rending than the *Liebestrod* of Isolde in the last act of *Tristan and Isolde* – if one's ear has adjusted to the five-tone scale. Once again, poor Kieu is in despair and goes once more to the river. Briefly, all of the characters parade before her as if she were reliving a flashback of her sad life. Then dancers in white appear with white silk streamers with which they artfully create rippling waves. Gradually, Kieu sinks beneath the waves, one last delicate hand remaining, then only a flower . . .

There cannot have been a dry eye in the house.

To celebrate the Vietnamese New Year *(Tet)* while waiting for the performance of *Kieu*, I had gone to the new production, which translated as *The Strange Doctor*. Hong, the receptionist at my hotel, came with me and filled me in as the plot thickened, but the exaggerated characters and their antics would have been funny and easy enough to follow with no translation whatsoever. This was fall-about farce, akin to British pantomime and Gilbert and Sullivan. The music – two electric keyboards, an electric guitar and drums – although based on the traditional five-tone scale, sounded more or less modern and the knock-about male and female chorus lines of singers and dancers in glittering costumes were captivating.

Inspired by Moliere, *The Strange Doctor* had been adapted to make it contemporary with feudal life. The plot was about a peasant farmer, mistaken for a doctor, who is taken to the palace of the king to 'cure' the princess who cannot speak. Quite by accident, he does cure her, but along the way, there is much micky-taking of lesser officials, mandarin, puffed-up medics of assorted nationalities, lecherous philanderers and husbands who beat their wives. In that sort of company, naturally, the wives had to win. The hero and heroine, of course, were the farmer and his wife, who predictably decide that they far prefer to live the hard, simple life of their village rather than the complicated life of the palace. The audience loved it and we all tumbled out of the theatre, our faces aching from non-stop grinning for over two hours. All the world loves a lover, but even more, all the world loves a good laugh.

(Performances are irregular at the Golden Bell Theatre, 72 Hang Bac. Ask a Vietnamese to inquire, tel. 3825 7823).

HANOI THEN AND NOW

One often abandons the old for the new,
One often abandons the lamp for the moon
  – Vietnamese proverb

Consider the changes elderly Hanoians have witnessed in the past sixty years: life under French colonial rule, occupation by the Japanese during World War II, followed immediately by the Indo-Chinese War against the French, then ten years of conflict between the North and the South, leading to the Vietnam War, ending in reunification of the country in 1975. It is only during the last few decades that Hanoians have been at peace in order to rebuild their city and their country. And rebuild they have, with pent-up energy from a base of poverty and much destruction. To those who live in Hanoi, change may seem slow, but to the occasional visitor, the rapidity of change is quite breathtaking.

During my experience of Hanoi, there have been phenomenal changes. When I first came to Vietnam (1997), the streets were swarming with bicycles, there were very few motorbikes and even fewer cars and those belonged to either government officials, diplomats or foreigners business executives. The manager of one of Hanoi's luxury hotels at the time told me that six months earlier when he had first arrived, there had been only two taxi firms in Hanoi and in only six months, suddenly there were six. There seem to be countless taxi companies now – except on a rainy day when you need one – and nearly every major junction has its motorbike taxis *(xe on)* stationed at the corner to zoom pedestrians around the city more quickly.

In 2004, I noticed a sudden proliferation of motorbikes – 'cheap imports from China' – and by then, there were at least a dozen taxi companies. Now that everyone can own a motorbike right down to the hotel cleaner – Hanoi issues three hundred new licenses a month! – the new status symbol before buying a car is a motor scooter, despite their cost of several thousand dollars. And the Vietnamese have started buying cars, big ones, to carry the entire extended family.

Fewer cyclos ply for trade, sticking mainly to the tourist areas around Hoan Kiem lake, the Old Quarter and West Lake, but remain the very best form of transport for the tourist who wants to travel slowly and ogle in all directions at everything he passes without having to crane out of the windows.

When I first arrived, the only city buses I saw were old rattletraps, belching exhaust fumes. In 2008, I found a whole new fleet of city buses carrying commuters into the centre of the city, to their far-out factory jobs or to their homes in the new satellite cities – those who have not acquired motorbikes. Traffic has increased exponentially, to the point of paralysis. During one evening rush hour, I stood laughing on a street corner and watched as traffic progressively pressed tighter and tighter into the centre of the junction, no one willing to get way. But given Hanoi, that junction probably has a traffic light by now.

When I first came to Hanoi, there were very few traffic lights at all and those seemed to be largely ignored. No more. Traffic obediently comes to a halt when the lights turn red with only occasional hell-bent bicycles or motorbikes defying the law, sailing through the junction or around a corner. Major streets are much better lit at night. I remember striking off on foot across a very dark junction in the glare of a line-up of motorbike beams, wondering if I would make it across the street. Unlit bicycles at night used to be a menace. Even better since December 2007, safety helmets have become compulsory throughout the country, which should improve accident statistics.

In Hanoi, I have also noticed a certain easing of traffic through the creation of one-way streets. This may make a taxi's route a bit convoluted, but the increased ease of movement is well worth it.

Another thing that has forcibly struck me is how much better off Hanoians are since I first arrived. They are much better dressed. Rubber sandals have given way to proper shoes for nearly everyone, tights and high heels for trendy young girls and their mothers and the ultra-trendy jeans of a decade ago have been replaced by smart skirts or trousers. Only the bamboo pole-toting vendors from the country still wear flip-flops and only a very few grannies still wear silk pyjamas on the streets of Hanoi.

Everyone seems to have a mobile phone from teenager to granddad, from matron to monk. Internet shops have sprung up, replacing the popular photography and photocopying shops and they are always full of the young, playing computer games.

When I first came to Hanoi I remember being struck by how many people on the streets – shopkeepers, cigarette and lottery ticket vendors – sat reading books. No longer. Passing open-front houses, everyone has a television set to watch soap operas, disco dancing, or cartoons.

Just as I was leaving Hanoi in 1998, the new Trang Tien multi-storey shopping centre opened at the corner of Trang Tien and Dinh Tien Hoang. Its escalator, the first in Hanoi, was such a novelty that oldsters were anxiously standing at the bottom wondering quite how to get on. The kids were gleefully riding up and down. There were no supermarkets. Although they may not be the hypermarkets of the West, supermarkets of varying sizes are now scattered throughout the city and it is pleasant to find not just many of the products to which one is accustomed in the West, but depending on the year, sometimes much improved wine for export from Dalat. Multi-storey shopping arcades have proliferated. Escalators are no longer a novelty.

Also, when I first stayed in the Old Quarter of Thirty-Six Streets, I remember worrying about power blackouts when I was working at my computer. Occasionally they did occur, when there would be a knock at the door and a lit candle handed in. No more blackouts or very few.

On the subject of hotels, the standard of accommodation in modestly priced mini-hotels has improved immensely. Years ago, the air-conditioners were noisy old boxes in a window. Now they are quieter, slim-lined, mounted high on a wall and best of all, they pump out warm air in winter as well as cool air in summer. Only luxury hotels had heating ten years ago and I remember a foreign resident telling me that when she sent a Vietnamese friend to buy her a two-way air-conditioner that he came back with a one-way appliance, explaining that it was unhealthy to have artificial heat. Well, times have changed. Hanoians have discovered how pleasant it is to be cosy and warm in winter.

Luxury blocks of flats have gone up, dotted about the city.

Moreover, in a strident attempt to solve the need for accommodation of Hanoi's increasing population and pulsing high density, in the past few years new satellite suburbs, planned new towns, have shot up to the south-west of central Hanoi. To live in one is to instantly become a commuter. Nevertheless, the peace of wide streets, trees and spacious villas set apart in gardens as well as sleek, modern high-rise flats must seem appealing to families living in cramped quarters, however central.

Many more changes may not be immediately obvious to a visitor. Since the government reforms *(doi moi)* of 1986, Hanoi along with the rest of the country, has seen an easing of government controls and partial privatization of state-owned enterprises, including even state-owned banks; the proliferation of private banks; the encouragement of private enterprise and investment, both local and investment from abroad.

Vietnam's stock market was established in 2000, first in Ho Chi Minh City, then a second market in Hanoi. By late 2008, 332 firms had listed, 164 in Hanoi, 168 in HCMC, including partly privatized companies. The two markets operate separately. Listing requirements are slightly more stringent in HCMC; therefore, it is more prestigious to be listed there. An OCT market, UPCOM, is in its infancy and will probably be officially launched in 2009.

Vietnam's Chamber of Commerce and Investment reported that foreign direct investment in Vietnam reached sixty billion dollars (£40 bn) by November 2008, compared to twenty billion dollars (£13 bn) for 2007. Vietnam offers foreign investors a corporate tax holiday for the first four years and a corporate tax rate of only ten per cent for the next four years, appealing to companies looking for well-educated, cheap labour.

At an industrial park opened in 2000 near Hanoi's Noi Bai International Airport, forty-six factories already employ more than 16,000 workers.

Canon has a printer factory; Nisson is expanding its vehicle engineering centre; Hanesbrands, a US underwear company is setting up two new factories; Intel is building a one billion dollar microchip factory and General Electric opened its first plant in Vietnam in 2008 to make turbine components.

Attracted by lower wages in Vietnam than in China, the Texhong Textile Group from Shanghai has set up a factory; Ever-Glory, which sells to Walmart is here, as well as a Taiwanese shoe company employing 7,000 workers, exporting to Timberland and Prada. Mitsubishi Heavy Industries, the largest aerospace company in Asia, announced in November 2008 that it would build a factory in Hanoi to begin production in 2009, assembling wing flaps for Boeing's 737 in a 4,000-square-metre plant.

162

Also lured by the tax incentives and lower wages than in China, the Taiwanese Printed Circuit Association (TPCA) is planning to create in the next eight months (early 2009) a special exclusive zone near Hanoi to accommodate ten to twenty TPCA manufacturers on approximately seven hundred forty acres.

A fair chunk of foreign investment has gone into new hotels – and residential accommodation – aiming at the top end of the market. The new luxury Intercontinental Hotel opened near West Lake in December, 2007, bringing the total of Hanoi's five-star hostelries to nine: Sofitel Metropole, Hilton Opera, Nikko, Horizon, Sheraton, Daewoo, Melia and Sofitel Plaza.

Tourism has taken off. In 2007, Vietnam hosted 4.2 million foreign visitors, an increase of sixteen per cent on the previous year, nearly all of whom passed through Hanoi, pushing Vietnam up from sixth to fourth place in the league of the world's fastest-growing destinations.

Equally, the government has opened its doors to education. Two Australian universities, the Royal Melbourne Institute of Technology and Monash University, have already opened facilities in Hanoi. A German university and several South Korean technical colleges plan to open in HCMC and Nghe An Province. Meanwhile, families from the prime minister's down are sending their children to study abroad.

But happily, the things I hold most dear about Hanoi have not changed: the beauty and calm of Hoan Kiem lake, the scent of pavement *pho* stalls and of pavement grills roasting pork, the cries of early morning fruit vendors bouncing along with their bamboo carrying poles, the clutter and bustle of the Old Quarter, the flower vendors selling roses from the back of their bicycles, the young who socialize, sitting on tiny stools cracking sunflower seeds every evening opposite the cathedral, the pavement 'dust cafes' and the fresh beer *(bia hoi)* bars in Hang Hanh, the heady aroma of Vietnamese coffee at Bon Mua cafe, above all, the warmth and friendliness of Hanoi's kindly, gentle people. These precious things have not changed and I hope they never will.

Pleasant hours fly past
– Vietnamese proverb

HISTORIC APPENDIX

PREHISTORY

Earliest human habitation 500,000-300,000 years ago
    In 1965 archaeologists discovered teeth of an early
    anthropoid at Lang Son, near the Vietnam-China border.

Epipaleolithic Son Vi culture, 20,000-10,000 BC
    A subsequent discovery in the hills of Vinh Phu, 33 miles
    (53 km) northwest of Hanoi, provides a link with Mesolithic
    finds.

Two Mesolithic cultures, 11,000-8,000 BC, when humans began
to domesticate tuber vegetables:
    Hoa Binh, 11,000-10,000 BC
    Bac Son, 10,000-6,000 BC

Many regionally varied Neolithic and Bronze Age cultures,
4,000-600 BC

Hung kings of the Viet kingdom, 700-179BC
    The pre-history of the Viets is a blend of the myths of the
Hung kings, legendary descendants of the Dragon of the Seas and
the Fairy of the Mountains. Another legend describes the eternal
struggle against the devastating floods of the Red river delta as
the conflict between the Spirit of the Mountain and the Spirit of
the Waters for the hand of a beautiful princess.
    Van Lang, the 7th century BC embryonic state of the Hung
kings, was made up of a federation of 15 Viet tribes called the
Lac Viet. By the middle of the 3rd century BC, Lac Viet had been
annexed by An Duong Vuong, chief of the neighbouring
mountainous Viet kingdom called Au Viet. The new kingdom,
combining Au Viet and Lac Viet, became known as Au Lac. Its
capital was at Co Loa, north of Hanoi. An Duong Vuong was the
first of 18 Hung kings.

The culture of the Viets covered the entire Bronze Age and the beginning of the Iron Age, up to the beginning of recorded history. It is the Viets, also known as Kinh, who were the forebears of the 86 per cent, ethnic majority of the Vietnamese population today.

In 179 BC the Chinese warlord, Trieu Da (Chao To) conquered the Viet kingdom of Au Lac and became king of what he called Nam Viet, the Chinese name for South China. This was a prelude to Chinese colonization by the Han dynasty in 111 AD that was to dominate what has become North Vietnam for more than a thousand years.

Vietnam's present-day minorities still number 54 distinct ethnic groups, made up of a mixture of Mongoloids, who came from the north and the original Malayo-Polynesian inhabitants of the central coast and mountains.

VIETNAMESE HISTORY IN SIX EASY STEPS

I am indebted to Vietnamese scholar Huu Ngoc for his simplified division of Vietnam's convoluted history:

$$1000 + 1000 + 900 + 80 + 30 \text{ years}$$

1 Somewhat less than 1000 years BC, the formative period of the Viet civilisation in the Red river basin, Bronze Age.
2 More than 1000 years of Chinese domination, 179 BC to 938 AD, during which there were numerous insurrections against the Chinese.
3 Roughly 900 years of national independence, 938-1858, several national dynasties, territorial expansion to the south, cultural influence but resistance to invasion from China.
4 Approximately 80 years of French colonization, 1862-1945, the first French conquests date from 1858, the French-Japanese occupation from 1940-1945.
5 Then 30 years of war, the Wars of Independence 1945-1975: resistance to the French 1945-1954, ending at Dien Bien Phu; resistance to the Americans 1965-1975, ending at Saigon.
6 Since 1975, efforts to overcome social and economic crisis, the politics of renovation, *doi moi,* begun in 1986.

RECORDED HISTORY

Chinese domination 179 BC-938 AD
    Brief rule by Trung sisters 40-43 AD.
    Uprisings in the 3rd and 6th centuries.
    Defeat of the Chinese in 938 by Ngo Quyen at Bach Dang river.

Champa
Hindu kingdom of Champa appeared around Danang, late 2nd century AD. Champa included four ethnic groups, all belonging to the Austronesian race, first recorded in Chinese records as the nation of Lin Yi. It ranged along the coastline from Ngang Pass, (272 m, 439 km south of Hanoi), south to the province of Phan Rang. The Chams cultivated wet-rice and left traces of sophisticated irrigation systems as well as splendid carved statues and numerous brick temple complexes dedicated at various times from the 7th to 14th centuries to their matriarchal, Buddhist and Hindu gods. They were active traders from their ports at Hoi An near Danang and Thi Nai in Binh Dinh province, trading with India, Java, Arab countries, China, Japan, Spain and Portugal, the Netherlands and the France.

Funan
Indianised kingdom of Funan in southern Vietnam 1st to 6th centuries AD. Its capital port city, Oc-Eo in present-day Kien Giang province.

Chenla
Khmer kingdom of Chenla attacked Funan mid-6th century and absorbed Funan.

VIETNAMESE DYNASTIES
Ngo	939-965
Rule by the Twelve Lords	965-968
Dinh	968-980
Early Le	980-1009

Ly	1010-1225
Tran	1225-1400
Ho	1400-1407
Post-Tran	1407-1413
Chinese rule	1414-1427
Later Le	1428-1527 (nominally until 1788)
Mac	1527-1592
Trinh Lords (North)	1545-1778
Nguyen Lords (South)	1558-1778
Tay Son	1778-1802
Nguyen	1802-1945 (nominally after 1884)
French rule	1883-1945 (SouthVN a French colony from 1867)
Japanese occupation	1940-1945
Nominal independence	1945-1954 (French Indo-Chinese War 1945-1954)
Communist (North)	1954-1975 (Vietnam War 1965-1975)
Republic of VN (South)	1954-1975 (Ngo Dien Diem 1954-63)
Communist Reunification	1975

NGUYEN EMPERORS	REIGN	
First, Gia Long	1802-1819	Founder Nguyen dynasty
Second, Minh Mang	1820-1840	Major builder of Citadel
Third, Thieu Tri	1841-1847	Prolific poet died at 40
Fourth, Tu Duc	1848-1883	Longest reign 36 years
Fifth, Duc Duc	1883	Shortest rule 3 days,
Sixth, Hiep Hoa	1883	Ruled 4 months poisoned
Seventh, Kien Phuc	1883-1884	Ruled 7 months poisoned
Eighth, Ham Nghi	1884-1885	Aged 14 resisted French
	1885	French seized power
Ninth, Dong Khanh	1885-1889	French puppet died at 23
Tenth, Thanh Thai	1889-1907	Son of Duc Duc exiled
Eleventh, Duy Tan	1907-1916	Anti-French exiled
Twelfth, Khai Dinh	1916-1925	European style palace
Thirteenth, Bao Dai	1925-1945	Abdicated 1945 died in Paris 1997

BIBLIOGRAPHY

Hoang Kim Dang, (Introduction by Nguyen Khac Vien), *Vietnam Album,* The Gioi Publishers, Hanoi, 1991

Huu Ngoc, *Sketches for a Portrait of Vietnamese Culture,* The Gioi Publishers, Hanoi, 1997

Huu Ngoc and Borton, Lady, *Ha Noi's Old Quarter,* The Gioi, Hanoi, 2003

Huu Ngoc and Borton, Lady, *Cheo, Popular Threatre,* The Gioi, Hanoi, 2005

Huu Ngoc and Borton, Lady, *Pho, A Specialty of Ha Noi,* The Gioi, Hanoi, 2006

Huu Ngoc and Borton, Lady, *Sifting of French Architecture,* The Gioi, Hanoi, 2006

Huu Ngoc and Cohen, Barbara, *Tet,* The Gioi Publishers, Hanoi, 1997

Huu Ngoc and Borton, Lady, *Vietnamese Classical Opera,* The Gioi, Hanoi, 2006

Jamieson, Neil L., *Understanding Vietnam,* University of California Press, Oakland, California, 1995

Le Brusq, Arnauld, photographs Selva, Leonard, *Vietnam, A Travers l'Architecture Coloniale,* Patrimoines et Medias Editions de l'Amateur, Paris, 1999

Lewis, Norman, Omnibus: *The Dragon Apparent, Golden Earth, A Goddess in the Stones,* Picador/Macmillan General Books, London, 1996

Luu Minh Tri, *Heritage Sites and Beauty Spots in Hanoi and Northern Vietnamese Provinces,* The Gioi, Hanoi, 2002

Nguyen Khac Vien and Huu Ngoc, *Vietnamese Literature,* The Gioi, Hanoi, 1981

Nguyen The Long and Pham Mai Hung, *130 Pagodes de Hanoi,* The Gioi, Hanoi, 2002

Nguyen Vinh Phuc, *Ha Noi, Past and Present,* The Gioi, Hanoi, 2004

Nguyen Vinh Phuc, Hanoi, *Streets of the Old Quarter and Around Hoan Kiem Lake,* The Gioi, Hanoi, 2006

Unnamed author, *Van Mieu Quoc Tu Giam, The Temple of Literature,* The Gioi, Hanoi, 2004

CPSIA information can be obtained
at www.ICGtesting.com
Printed in the USA
LVHW080129280820
664409LV00021B/3081